FIND YOUR JOY AND RUN WITH IT

ROSIE MANKES

A gift from a friend at Deep Creek Lake,
Pan Scott
Q A. 21, 2020

AROMAN PUBLICATIONS

Find Your Joy and Run With It

© Copyright 2018 by Rosie Mankes
Aroman Publications

All rights reserved. This book or any portion thereof may not be reproduced or used in any manner whatsoever without the express written permission of the publisher except for the use of brief quotations in a book review.

Printed in the United States of America
First Printing, 2020
ISBN 9798666866795

https://www.rosiemankes.com

Cover Photo By Guillaume Bolduc on Unsplash

CONTENTS

Author's Note	vii
Acknowledgements	ix
Dear Reader...	xiii

1. How it all started — 1
2. September 15th, 2015 — 3
3. Ouch! — 7
4. The phone call — 9
5. Pedicure — 11
6. February 2018 — 13
7. Marianne — 20
8. November 2015 – back to the breast cancer journey — 24
9. Mom — 26
10. Transitioning? — 28
11. Showtime — 32
12. 1-800-Flushme — 35
13. January 4th, 2016 — 39
14. Help me! — 42
15. Mom again — 47
16. The night before — 49
17. Marianne — 51
18. Today's the day — 55
19. Who knew? — 59
20. February 1st, 2016 – It's really showtime — 62
21. Recovery room — 64
22. Sleep time — 66
23. The drains — 69
24. Settling in — 72
25. Results — 74

26. What a cluster-fuck!	76
27. The Positano	79
28. Who's Looking at YOU?	81
29. Dimes	87
30. Reconstruction	91
31. Road trip	93
32. What are family and friends?	95
33. Mom again	96
34. Loss	99
35. Who am I?	103
36. So good?	108
37. House cleaning	110
38. Tattoos	112
39. Venting a bit	117
40. Checkmate!	119
41. Completely devastating!	121
42. A gathering	126
43. Carl's memorial service	128
44. Repast	131
45. Carl and my mother	134
46. A package arrived	136
47. Therapy	140
48. Reflection	141
49. Marianne again	145
50. Homework	146
51. More dimes	149
52. Nothing like a new baby	150
53. Processing grief	153
54. Reminiscing	155
55. FaceTime chat	157
56. Sadness	159
57. A small window	161
58. Time for another wedding!	163
59. Things I would miss if I died	166
60. Meditation	175

61. Pondering	177
62. Let it be	179
63. Another step forward	182
64. A sobering sunrise	184
65. The note	186
66. Update	188
67. Flight time	190
68. Visiting with Mom	192
69. When I began to turn the corner	194
70. Private dance lessons with Dan	200
71. Sneakers	202
72. Public speaking training	204
73. The Rainbow Room	207
74. Life Coaching	211
75. Mindfulness	213
76. June 5th, 2018	216
77. The Renewal – June 5th, 2018	218
78. Update on Mom	221
79. Life Coach Rosie!	222
80. The next day	225
Epilogue: Marianne	226
About the Author	228

AUTHOR'S NOTE

This is an inspirational Memoir with some fictionalized components and future projections. Only first or abbreviated names have been used. When first and last names are used, they have been changed to protect the privacy of the character.

ACKNOWLEDGEMENTS

I have many to thank!

First, I need to thank my husband, Dan, who has been by my side through this entire experience helping and supporting me even when I did not think I had an ounce of energy in me to continue on. I love you, Dan! Of course, I must thank my sons, Greg and Jordan. Our sons are the greatest gifts we have received during our 32 years of marriage. Our boys and Greg's girlfriend Allie have said repeatedly through this unbelievable journey, "You got this. You are the strongest person we know."

Gratitude doesn't begin to describe how I feel about my family and friends that have hopped onto the Rosie Mankes Crazy Train and stayed with me all through the ride: My friends Noreen, Maribel, Annie, Lori, and Geri, who were my very first cheerleaders and fans of my book, encouraging me to keep writing even when I questioned if I could pull this off and share my story. My beautiful niece, Ciana, my brother Carl's daughter, has supported this project from the very beginning. Each week,

ACKNOWLEDGEMENTS

we would hop on a call and discuss next steps. I am immensely grateful for this time spent together on this.

I also need to thank Susan, Donna, Bonnie, Adria, Mara, Trish, Dina, Sara, Doreen, Nancy, Rosemary, Maria, Lori, my Hazlet peeps, and my cousins Joanne, Maria and Toni Ann. Then there are my nieces Emily, Hannah, Ariel, Sarah and Rachel and my in-laws. All these people have played a part in my healing and I am forever grateful to them.

A special shout-out to my cousin Lisa, who toured many assistant living facilities with me when I was desperately searching for a suitable place for my mom to live. After many disappointing visits, Lisa found the perfect place, one that matched all the criteria I was looking for and that I can proudly call home for my mom.

My life coach and mentor, Dr. Michele D'Amico, helped me through my surgical journey and Dr. Mindy Breyer took me on as a patient when I was so very broken and week by week helped me to find my way back to becoming Rosie again. And Loretta, my friend since first grade, who spent time on the phone with me every night during the most challenging year of my life, and who I spoke to every Thursday on my way to therapy with Dr. Breyer.

I want to thank Dan Angel, Founder of Fezziwig Studios, and a multiple Emmy, Peabody and WGA award-winning writer and producer, who believed in my story when it was just a few blogs, encouraged me to write a book, and made several introductions for potential collaborations. I would also like to thank Brian Gott, who leads Innovation at the Entertainment Industry Foundation, the creator of Stand Up 2 Cancer, for also believing in my story and supporting my efforts to share it with others.

ACKNOWLEDGEMENTS

A special shout out to my long-time friend, Peggy Mansfield, who read my manuscript in 24 hours and became an avid supporter from the very beginning. I especially loved our quarantine Zoom Cocktail Hours where we spent time catching up and discussing marketing strategies for the book launch!

I also need to thank Maria Svinos for doing a great job managing my social media and for creating a book cover for me that perfectly conveys the feel I had hoped for when new readers hold the book in their hands. A special shout-out to Abby Vigdor for putting together and helping execute a robust, awesome, creative book launch! You rock, Abby!

I need to thank John Bolin, who came into my life helping me with formatting and the self-publishing process when I was frantically trying to get the book completed.

THANK YOU to my mother for instilling in me strength, resilience, and courage and for teaching me to never give up on my dreams. I love you Mom!

To Marianne – especially for her "winks," Carl, Kathy, Tommy and all of the other family members we have lost through the years. You will always be in my heart and am so very thankful that you were a part of my life.

DEAR READER...

"Sometimes you just have to hang on and trust that life's storms are carrying you to better shores." – JANE LEE LOGAN

1

HOW IT ALL STARTED

For as long as I can remember, I've always cried at weddings when the bride walks down the aisle. There's something magical and very emotional about the organ music becoming a bit louder, everyone standing to honor the woman in the beautiful, white gown being escorted to the alter to meet her soon-to-be husband. As she passes each person, all eyes are on her, there's so much promise in what lies ahead for the two of them, as they begin their future together.

Over the past couple of years, I began crying during another part of the ceremony—when the couple exchange vows. I look at each bride, many wearing low-back, V-cut gowns, same as I wore, and I think about myself, so many years ago, standing beside Dan and saying those words we all know by heart: "I, Rosemarie, take thee Daniel to be my husband..."

The part of the vows that chokes me up the most now is when the couple say, "in sickness and in health 'til death do us part." Dan and I have really test-driven these vows during our marriage. I look at the bride and groom holding hands, face-to-face, exchanging these words of promise to each other, and I think back to the 24-year-old me about to embark on our journey. Nothing could have prepared us for what lay ahead—the blessings, celebrations, love, the memories we made, but also the sickness and sorrow. I also look at the beautiful young backs of these women, their skin so youthful and untarnished, and I think about the scars from my lung cancer surgery that would now be visible in a dress like that. I think about my other scars from my double mastectomy that are always covered by my bra but are now permanently a part of my life. I wonder about life, the triumphs, the challenges, and the highs and lows that we all have ahead of us as we start out and how we do what we need to do to make it through them all. Here's my story.

2

SEPTEMBER 15TH, 2015

The phone rang at 6:00 a.m. I answered it with a hoarse voice, "Hello?"

My 85-year-old mother answered, "Rosemarie, I just wanted to tell you that I'm not moving to New Jersey. I'm staying in Brooklyn!"

"Mom, it's really early in the morning. Can we talk about this later today?"

"OK," she replied. "I'm sorry I woke you."

I struggled to reach over to hang up the phone. I sighed.

My husband Dan asked, "How many times did she call tonight?"

I replied, "That was the third time."

Dan said, "Even with her dementia, the one thing she remembers is our phone number!"

I responded, "Yep!" and roll over and try to get back to bed.

Who am I kidding, I was up! At this point, I was done trying to sleep, so I reached for my phone. I checked Facebook for a couple of minutes, looked at emails, and then texted my BFF Noreen because I knew she was an early riser. Our standard text during early morning or later in the evening to see if we are available is, "Talk?"

Five minutes later she responded: "Yes."

I was so exhausted. My siblings and I were trying to transition my mom into an assisted living facility because, as her dementia advanced, it became too difficult for her to live alone anymore. This was not going well at all as my mom did not want to leave her home in Brooklyn to enter a facility in New Jersey.

I called Noreen and said, "Hey."

She replied, "How are you, my love?"

"Terrible. I needed to cancel today's appointment. My mom called me three times in the middle of the night to let me know that she is *not* under any circumstances leaving Brooklyn to move to the assisted living facility near me in Jersey. I'm sorry to do this to you, but I'm going to have to postpone my mammogram until January, after my mother hopefully settles in."

Noreen, my no-nonsense sensible friend, said to me, "Don't be ridiculous! I'll drive, and you can take a cat nap in the car. Your mom has been making you crazy for weeks about this moving crap! What you need is to get your head away from this stuff and have a nice lunch with your girlfriends."

Our other BFF Maribel was coming along for the ride—and the lunch date of course. I reluctantly agreed, showered, got ready, and later that morning off we went for our 45-minute drive to our routine appointment and lunch date.

It was a beautiful sunny day, and Noreen and I had our annual mammograms scheduled for 10:30 and 11:00 a.m. in Essex County, New Jersey. We always scheduled our next yearly screening just prior to leaving the breast imaging center after we got the all clear sign from the radiologist and paid our co-pay. For the past five years, it had become a ritual to get our boobies checked and then head out to a nice lunch, sitting at an outdoor café in town.

Everything went as scheduled. Noreen went in first, and I flipped through a magazine and checked out what was happening on Facebook to pass the time. Then Noreen came out, and it was my turn. So much has been written about mammograms, but I would just like to add one observation that I haven't heard yet. To me, a mammogram is like a sick game of Twister where the tech makes you position and contort your body in ways that are so unnatural. At one moment, one arm is here, the other is here, your head is tilted and turned upward and away from the machine, and you're leaning in almost on your tippy toes, twisting your hips so that all your breast is in the machine. Then BAM! They squash your boob into a pancake and tell you "Don't move and don't breathe." Fun! Then it's time for the other breast.

I made my way to the holding area, so the radiologist could review my films. After a while, I was told that an ultrasound would be required. This was not unusual for me because, even though I'm a small B-cup, I have been told for years that I have very dense, cystic breasts that usually require further delving to rule out any problems.

When the ultrasound was completed, I started to put my clothes on.

The tech knocked on the door and said, "Rosemarie, the radiologist, Dr. L, wants to see you when you're finished getting dressed."

Again, I felt no real concern, as this was routine for me. I've been to her office many times over the years, with her pointing out one lump or another that they wanted to keep an eye on or do a needle biopsy on, and, thus far, nothing has ever come of it.

Today, Dr. L had my mammogram films on her large computer screen, and she pointed out four dots running across my breasts in an arch. The first thing I thought was that it looked like Orion's Belt, when you look at the constellation up in the sky on a clear night.

Dr. L explained, "Rosemarie, you see these four dots?" She pointed to each with the tip of her pen. "These are calcifications. I don't feel there is any reason to be concerned or alarmed, but my suggestion is that we biopsy each of them." Again, I've been down the biopsy road before, so I didn't feel much in the way of worry. Dr. L continued, "It's likely nothing to worry about. Usually with calcifications such as these, there is an 80/20 percent chance against it being cancer."

"Those odds sound pretty good," I said. "Should I schedule the biopsies for next week?"

She said, "Yes, let's get you in as soon as possible. With everything you've been through with your lung cancer and surgery, let's get this done so you can have peace of mind."

We agreed to schedule the biopsy for September 24th. I paid the bill, and my friends and I headed to lunch.

3

OUCH!

These biopsies were not like the others I'd done before. They were stereotactic biopsies, where instead of extracting fluid from a cyst or potential tumor to run it through a lab, they took a tissue sample. However, no one shared with me that it would be like having a nail gun shot into your breast without any advance notice. The tech was strictly business-like and told me, "Rosemarie, I need you to lie on your stomach, put your head in the hole"—which was cut out like a massage table—"and don't move."

Soon after, Dr. L arrived and put a vice grip on my breast and then boom—AND I MEAN BOOM—she hit me with this SHARP SHOT TO THE BREAST, extracting tissue that made me, not a wimp for pain, yell out "Fuck! That hurt!!!" when it occurred. I had a huge bruise for three weeks after this procedure, but, in retrospect, this was the least of my problems.

Next came the wait. It was Friday, and I would get the results on Monday. As I always did when faced with anxiety-riddled situations, I filled my time with things and activities to keep me busy. We had dinner plans with friends on Saturday night and went to a street festival with live music on Sunday. My son, Jordan, at this point a junior in college, called us when we were attending the festival and was very distraught. His good friend had been fundraising out of town with a bunch of kids for his school and tragically died in a car accident. As parents, our hearts were filled with grief for this family, and we tried to console our son. He shared that his friend's sorority sisters were putting together a GoFundMe site to try to raise funds for the family. As it turned out, the GoFundMe site hit the internet on Sunday night, the night of her death, with a goal of raising $1,000, and, by Tuesday, they shut it down because it had raised approximately $40,000. So many people were overcome with grief as a result of this tragic accident that they rushed to help by contributing to her fund.

4

THE PHONE CALL

Having been in sales for so many years and having to accept rejection and victories on a regular basis, I can always tell immediately from a person's tone of voice whether what they're about to tell me is going to be positive or negative. So, when Dr. L called me on Monday morning with the results of the biopsy, I knew it wasn't going to be good.

As it turned out, it wasn't terrible, but I knew from the intonation in her voice that the 80/20 thing didn't work out in my favor. "Rosemarie," she shared with me, "you have stage zero cancer in your left breast, which, if you're going to have breast cancer, is the best stage to have. It's also called DCIS, ductal carcinoma in situ."

By definition, DCIS is the presence of abnormal cells inside a milk duct in the breast. DCIS is considered the earliest form of breast cancer and is noninvasive, meaning it hasn't spread out of the milk duct to invade other parts of the breast. Most of us know that the word carcinoma means cancer, but I didn't know that in situ means it is contained and has not spread.

As I was trying to process what this meant and learn Latin at the same time, I just remembered thinking that I was "fucked". I couldn't catch a break, first lung cancer at 44 and now breast cancer at 52. I don't mean to compare or judge, but many of my friends had never even been hospitalized, let alone had cancer, so I was feeling a bit depressed and angry about the cards I'd been dealt as a two-time cancer patient waiting to see what's ahead for me.

Dr. L said, "You're going to need to have a lumpectomy, but before that, I want you to have an MRI on your right breast to make absolutely sure they haven't missed any possibility of cancer in this breast because we also found some abnormal cells there as well." All of this was agreed upon and scheduled. I hung up and sat for a moment to process what lay ahead for me. I picked up the phone to call Dan to share the news. I cannot say that I wasn't having a pity "why me" party at this moment, but then something real and honestly raw hit me. I thought about Jordan's friends' mom, who just yesterday received a call that her daughter was killed in a horrible car crash, and I said to myself, "You know what, Rosie? I would take my call over that mother's call any day of my life."

5

PEDICURE

My friend Maribel asked me if I wanted to get out tomorrow for a little while. "Why don't we go for a pedicure, Rosa?" Maribel asked. "It'll make you feel better."

"That sounds like fun," I said. "I'd love to get out of the house to break up the day and not think about this cancer stuff and all of the testing for a little while."

"Perfect," she said. "What time works for you"?

"I don't know, how about 1:00 p.m.?"

Maribel agreed to make the appointment and pick me up. Maribel was my loving, pampering friend. She came over every couple of days to wash and blow out my hair when I had my lung surgery in 2008 because she knew I couldn't do it myself, and she wanted me to look beautiful during a time I felt so helpless. She, among many of my friends and family, are my angels on earth.

We arrived at the place just a little prior to our appointment time, took off our coats, and sat down. The owner of the spa motioned Maribel and I over to side-by-side pedicure chairs. We took off our flip flops and sat down to soak our feet in the bubbling Jacuzzi spa. "Ah," I said, "this feels great! It's been so long since I had a pedicure."

"You see, Rosa? You just need a little pampering sometimes!"

We were then interrupted by two Asian women, who came over to take our feet out of the Whirlpool bath and turn it off. My lady turned to me and said, "Excuse me, this first pedicure?"

"No," I said. "It's just been a long time since the last one."

"Your feet, very dry and cracked."

"Well, I've been going through a lot recently, so I haven't had the opportunity to take care of these things."

"Toenails, you cut or bite?"

"Excuse me?"

"You cut or bite toenails?" The Asian woman lifted her foot toward her mouth to demonstrate how you might bite your toenails.

"CUT!!" I shouted.

"Because my daughter, she seven years old, and she bites."

"I think I'm a little old for that!"

The Asian woman then walked away to get more materials for the pedicure. I turned and said to Maribel, "Am I crazy or did she just ask me if I bite my toenails?"

Maribel laughed. "Yes. She did."

I shook my head and threw my hands up in disbelief.

6

FEBRUARY 2018

*S*kipping forward to approximately two-and-a-half years after my exceedingly challenging journey began, I gave my first speech as a motivational speaker...

"*The crazy thing about my becoming a motivational speaker is that I distinctly knew it was my calling to be one, but I have a little secret. I have a bit of stage fright. So, I find that if I tell a funny story before launching into my topic, it helps me push through. So here goes:*

When my younger son Jordan was little and stayed home from school because he was sick, we had this ritual. We made the doctor's appointment, and sometime before or after we headed to the doctor, we went to the pet store to play with puppies. As you know, if you're a parent, even if your child has a fever and needs to go to the doctor, once the Motrin kicks in, they feel a bit better. And what's more awesome than having puppies jump around and play with you when you're having a bad day!

As we prepared to leave home, we had a power outage in our house, which meant my garage door openers weren't working. I tried as hard as I could to pull the manual cord on the garage door where my car was parked, but the garage door wouldn't pop. I called my husband, but he was in a meeting, so I couldn't ask him for help. That's when I had a Rosie Mankes moment. You see, at the time, we had a three-car garage, and my car was parked in the middle spot. I asked my son to help me move things around because, in my brain, I was going to make a U-turn in the garage and get us out via the left or right garage door, which were opening just fine. My son looked at me like I was crazy. Even at nine years old, this didn't seem possible to him, but, like me, he wanted to play with the puppies sometime before or after the doctor's visit. So, there I was, making maneuver after maneuver in the garage trying to turn the car around so I could get it out of one of the other doors. What was even more insane was that, at the time, I drove a minivan. Any reasonable person would logically understand this was virtually impossible to do.

I managed to get the van parallel to the garage door, at which point I was dripping with sweat. At that point, two of my friends, Annie and Noreen, randomly showed up, looked at me in the garage—again, my van was now parallel to the garage doors—and, with horrified looks on their faces, Annie said, "Rosie, what the hell are you doing?"

Reality set in that this was perhaps one of the stupidest things I had ever done. Fear suddenly rushed over me. I began to worry I might not be able to get the car back where it originally was because, if not, my husband was going to kill me. A visual flashed through my mind of my husband coming home, freaking out, seeing firefighters wielding their hydraulic jaws of life, sawing the van in half. What the hell did I do . . . ugh!

Yes, after quite some time, I heroically managed to get the car back in its proper place, and, amazingly, five minutes later, the power went back on. We were able to get out of the garage the proper way. We were off to the doctor's office and to play with puppies!

Here's my point: Sometimes we start on a path, and, as we're making our way through, it becomes emotionally and physically draining and unrealistic, and then we have to reevaluate and move to another path. But this doesn't negate the fact that, in the moment, we don't think it's erroneous or, in my case, insane. We simply realize at some point that we need to try to get out of this situation and go with another option.

Let me introduce myself: My name is Rosie Mankes. I'm a lung and breast cancer survivor. In a one-year time period from September of 2015 to September of 2016, my siblings and I had to transition my mother into an assisted living facility due to her declining health and the progression of her dementia. This was extremely difficult as she was very confused, incredibly fearful and resistant. She did NOT want to move from Brooklyn to New Jersey —which was where I live. More importantly, she did not want to lose the only life she knew, or her independence. At the same time, I was diagnosed with an early stage breast cancer after going through multiple biopsies and lumpectomies. A short time thereafter, I tested positive for a more recently discovered breast cancer mutation called Chek2, which put me at over a 50 percent chance of developing a more advanced stage breast cancer. I had a double mastectomy in February 2016 and reconstructive surgery in May of the same year. Just as things were beginning to settle down in September, I received a phone call that my 58-year-old healthy brother died from a horrific, tragic accident. My brother Tommy died in 1993, and now we needed to say goodbye to my only other brother Carl? How could this happen?

This was completely earth-shattering news, and, when combined with all of the other things I had encountered that year, I started to live my life in fear, actual paralyzing anxiety—mostly because I was terrified of what might happen next, especially as it related to my children or my husband Dan. I wasn't sure how to make it out of bed each morning and be me or pretend to be me. It was just awful.

Let me back up a bit: After my breast cancer diagnosis, I decided I was going to become a life coach. Anyone who knows me will tell you that, once I make a commitment to something, I throw myself in head and feet first. Two weeks after my mastectomy, I was enrolled in a program and had begun my coursework.

My friend Noreen said, "Most people who have major surgery binge watch Netflix. Only you go back to school and start a new business."

All through this journey, having also survived lung cancer in 2008 when I was just 44, I knew there was a reason my higher power was keeping me here. I was meant to do more than just curl up in a ball. I needed to somehow change from being a survivor to a thriver. I decided to make a plan that would allow me to move from fear and adversity to emotional wellness. I made a commitment to myself to re-purpose my life and gain strength and insight from the curveballs life threw at me.

To begin this transition, I started to purposely turn the earlier feelings I mentioned inside out and believe in and see, not just visually but also emotionally, spiritually, and physically, all of what life has to offer and to unlock what was inside of me, allowing me to live again. Self-care, self-examination, meditation, staying present and mindful, discrediting self-limiting beliefs, creating meaningful, action-oriented affirmations for myself, paying attention to nature and beauty, and, if you believe in the beyond, to feel and acknowledge little 'winks' and messages from those who have left us. These are just a few of the things that unfolded when I rolled up my sleeves and did the work. THIS IS WHY I'M HERE, to take what I have learned to help others who are limping through life, just trying to survive, and show them how to turn surviving into thriving. Moving from fear and adversity to emotional wellness!

I have written a book about my experience, Find Your Joy and Run with It, and I hope to have it published soon. One of the most rewarding parts of this journey has been the comments I have heard many times. People have said to me that they have searched and searched the internet, feeling helpless and despondent. Then they said, they 'found me' via my blogs or my website, and 'I was what they had been searching for, for such a long time.' When we spoke, they said that, I 'got them.' Perhaps the reason I 'got them' was because I had to get and figure myself out first!

Circling back to the garage story, sometimes we start on one path, realize it's not really working for us, maybe it's even a little insane, and then we need to reevaluate, revise, and repurpose our plan. So, let's talk about how you can do as I have and work toward finding your joy and running with it. (At this point in the presentation and with the audience's participation, we started to build a list of things I had done and things they could do to move from their current state to one with more peace, clarity, and vision for the future.)

I concluded the night with this:

So, now I have a little story to tell you about dimes.

Two years ago, I decided to put a dime, heads up, in my left shoe every day to remind me that I'm on the path I was meant to be on. It feels like a rock in my shoe, subtly annoying and nagging, but, instead of being upset by it, it inspires me.

Before you start thinking that I'm a bit bizarre, let me explain. As I mentioned earlier, I needed to make sense of why I was still here after two cancer diagnoses; my brother's sudden, unexpected death; having to put my mom into an assisted living facility that took her independence away; and what it is that I can give to those who are struggling. Being a life coach and motivational speaker seemed like the most natural place for me to work with people who are experiencing adversity and can't find their way. I believe I can help them identify their inner strength and build their core so they can feel empowered and alive again.

Moving from surviving to thriving, from adversity to emotional wellness. Yes, that is what I want to do: help people get there. This is something I've had to learn about for myself, both personally and professionally.

Why the dime in the shoe? As I was making my way through life coach training, graduating, and starting to work with clients, one day I found six dimes. Not being a person who carries change, it seemed unfathomable that I would find six dimes in a 24-hour period. Being curious, I Googled the meaning of this, and a couple of articles said the following: **Finding dimes is guidance or validation from your guardian angels that you're on the right path.**

Each day, as I continue to help people to find tranquility, wholeness, and healing, I become more certain of my path. Thriving instead of surviving! My intention is to inspire and motivate you. Perhaps you might like to also carry a dime to remind you to continue moving forward, feeling hopeful and confident that it's possible to turn things around. Please feel free to take a dime on the way out tonight. They're in a basket at the back of the room. Thank you for allowing me to share my story!"

∼

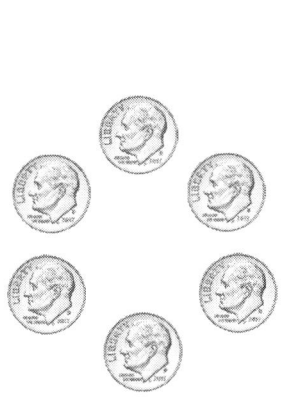

7

MARIANNE

I have an angel, and her name is Marianne. She wasn't always my angel; she was once my close friend. But, for whatever reason, God needed her when she was just shy of her 45th birthday and took her to heaven away from her young children, husband, family, and friends. To me and so many others, we felt dismay, anger, and questioning as to why she had to leave us. Before she left, she made some promises. She promised she would show us she was with us by providing us signals or, as my friend Mimi calls them, "winks from beyond." She promised that, if a glass broke at a gathering, that was her letting us know she was with us. She promised she would come to us via songs that we knew and loved to sing and listen to together, and countless times these songs have been playing in a store, restaurant, or on the radio at just the moment we might need to hear it. She would also come in the form of dragonflies passing by or simply being on jewelry of people we encountered, or via sunflowers, which were her favorite.

Throughout this journey, it became apparent that Marianne was next to me, helping me get up when I was most fearful that I couldn't take another step forward and make it through my day. Just a day, until the next, when perhaps things might get a little easier. One afternoon, just a few months after my brother Carl passed away, after my mastectomy and having to transition my mom into the assisted living facility, I was in a really bad place. I was wondering whether I could continue on. So much had happened this year. I was so filled with grief, but what was most concerning was that I was riddled with anxiety as to what was coming next. I felt cursed and, once again, consumed with fear that something would happen to Dan, or worse, my children.

To distract myself, I decided to clean out my bedroom closet in preparation for putting our house on the market. After my brother Carl's death, and with Dan and I being empty nesters, I made a complete and total about-face and stopped fighting my husband about downsizing to a simpler, less costly, and more maintenance-free residence. I was ready to move on. When I started working on the closet, I noticed there was a birthday bag tucked in the corner of the top shelf. I got on a step-up stool to pull it down and check what was inside. That was when I saw the note. You see, my friend Marianne passed away three weeks prior to my surprise 40th birthday celebration. She tried her best to live long enough to attend the surprise party Dan had planned for me. Unfortunately, she passed on February 12th, 2004, and my party was scheduled for March 6th of that year. She died just a few weeks before my party. The note I found was from her mother. This is what it said:

Rosie,

One day Marianne asked to have her jewelry box brought to her. She wanted to pick out something special for your "40th" birthday. She told me what box to put it in and how to wrap it. So here it is. Now, don't be sad, Rosie. Marianne wants you to "Find your joy and run with it."

I cried for quite some time that day. I remembered the present, beautiful pearl earrings, which I have been wearing every day since I discovered this note, but I hadn't remembered Marianne's mom's note when it was sent it, as I was so overcome with grief during that time.

After finding the note, I decided to make this my new mantra, and, through this journey, whether it might be a shitty or good day, I write down these words in my journal in the hopes that, one day, someday I will not be sad. One day, I'll *find my joy and run with it.*

FIND YOUR JOY AND RUN WITH IT

> Roxy,
>
> One day Marianne asked to have her jewelry box brought to her. She wanted to pick out something special for your "40th" Birthday.
>
> She told me what box to put it in and how to wrap it.
>
> So here it is.
>
> Now, don't be sad, Roxy, Marianne wants you to find your "Joy" and run with it.

Note from Marianne's mom

8

NOVEMBER 2015 – BACK TO THE BREAST CANCER JOURNEY

I was bleeding money. I was out of network with my current practice, and I was writing checks for hundreds of dollars, even thousands at one point, for multiple scans, MRIs, biopsies, and lumpectomies. After the diagnosis of stage zero breast cancer, I asked the doctor in charge of my breasts at the time, "Why me?"

To which she responded, "I don't know, Rosemarie. You just have shitty breasts."

This answer, coupled with the financial burden we were incurring, was the impetus to change practices! I went to my "go to" friends to find another doctor, and, luckily, I managed to find one that was in-network. All files and images were transferred to the new practice. We met with Dr. C on a Friday at 4:30 p.m. My friends that know her told me that this was the time she commonly meets with her cancer patients.

After reviewing my file and answering all our questions, she said, "The best course of action, in my opinion, is radiation treatment on your left breast for 10 weeks and careful screening. However, before any of this starts, we will need to get the results of the genetic testing to rule out any cancer gene mutation."

"What gene would you be looking for?" I asked.

"Well," she said, "your odds of carrying the BRCA gene are small because you're Italian. This genetic mutation is more commonly found in people of Eastern European Jewish descent. I just want to run the panel to make sure you're not a carrier, based on your history of having lung cancer."

I kept staring at something on her windowsill as I listened to her speak. Finally, I said, "You like sunflowers?" I pointed to them.

She responded, "Yes, I love sunflowers."

Without getting into details with her, I just said, "Me too!" and looked at my husband, who knew exactly what I was thinking. This was my first sign that Marianne was with me and that I had made the right decision to change practices and be under the care of Dr. C.

Her office scheduled the appointment with the genetic counselor, we paid our more-than-reasonable co-pay of $50.00, and we were out the door.

9

MOM

From 2014 to 2015, there was a huge decline in my mother's physical and mental health. I remember, during one visit to her house, she was face planted, unconscious, on her kitchen table. This was at a time when she was still in charge of planning out her daily medications. I quickly looked at the Monday-through-Sunday med vials and realized that, due to her dementia, she had put two Lunesta plus an Oxycodone pill in each days' pill regimen. This was bad, life threatening, and it needed to be fixed! Shortly thereafter, our family decided to get her a day companion to help assist with issues like this, as well as some cooking and driving.

One of the hardest things I've ever had to do was take my mom to a neurologist, have him give her a cognitive test, and tell her she was no longer fit to drive. We knew that this had to be done for her safety and the safety of others, but we needed a doctor to sanction this with an official test and report. This resulted in countless arguments, with a lot of distress and anxiety on her part.

"How dare he do this to me!" she said. "I'm going to get a lawyer and fight this!"

I tried reasoning with her, telling her that, with the companion, there was no need to drive anymore, but she could be a very stubborn and inflexible person to deal with at times. It was very difficult, and, unfortunately, I was the one who had to take her independence away from her by breaking it to her that she was no longer fit to drive. This was all done for the right reasons, but it still sucked. This went on for quite some time, with many angry calls from her and a lot of time trying to soothe her.

She was hospitalized several times that year, once with her hemoglobin levels going so low that the doctor in the ER shook his head, wondering why she was still alive. That day I practically carried her out of her house, after pleading with her that she needed to go to the hospital. She kept running to her bedroom, telling me, "Please, Rosemarie, I don't want to go to the hospital. I just want to lie down." I drove straight to New Jersey, to the place I felt would be best to potentially save her, and I checked her in.

It became apparent that she needed to be closer to us in a facility that knows how to take care of issues like this. My breast problems started at the same time, and, with my sibling living out of town either full or part time, I needed to know there was staff who could tend to her needs in a way I was no longer capable of doing. That's when we collectively decided she needed to transition from her house in Brooklyn to an assisted living facility in New Jersey.

10

TRANSITIONING?

"I WANT TO GO HOME! LET'S GO, ROSEMARIE! GET ME OUT OF HERE NOW!!" That was how my day started on December 4th, 2015.

As my mother's health and mind deteriorated, we decided she could no longer live alone in Brooklyn. I searched and visited every assisted living facility in our area to try and find a suitable, acceptable place for her to live. Of course, everything looks wonderful on the web until you pull up and enter the front door.

So many things come at you at once: the smell of urine, residents ambling by with walkers or wheelchairs, many sitting in the common area staring off into space or sleeping in a slumped over position. When I scheduled appointments with each place, I asked to visit during an activity time or social hour so I could see the residents interacting together. My mom was very friendly, so I knew that she would need to make friends for this transition to work.

After countless, disappointing visits, my cousin Lisa and I visited a facility, and she had the foresight to say, "This is nice, but a little dated. Where's your newest community?" Unbeknown to us, they were building a beautiful facility in my hometown, and Lisa and I headed straight to the sales office, located in a trailer. I liked the idea of my mom moving to a new place, with staff who would be eager to please and residents wanting to make friends. Plus, they had a social hour every day at 4:00 pm. Quoting my cousin, "Ro, if you have to put your mother in a place like this, pick a place where she can have daily cocktails!" They showed us a rendering of the building. It was beautiful, and we were sold. After discussing this with my siblings and doing a bit more research together, we were the first family to put a deposit on a unit in the facility. This began the transition for her move to New Jersey. At this point, I realized a dramatic shift had occurred—we were now the parents, and she was the child.

The director of the assisted living place we had selected for my mom said I was being silly when I told her that my mother was going to give them a hard time about moving in. "She'll be fine, Rosie. I've been doing this for over 25 years, and the residents usually give some push-back when they first move in. After a couple of weeks, they're fine. They adjust very nicely."

My brother Carl flew up from his home in South Carolina a couple of days before to help pack my mom's place up, assist with the move-in, and acclimate her to her new place. Throughout the week, we had been negotiating with her, trying to reason with her as to why it was necessary to move out of Brooklyn and closer to me in New Jersey. Obstinacy and dementia are two very tricky things to deal with simultaneously. My mother told my siblings and I: "I'm not moving to

New Jersey. I'm staying in Brooklyn, Brooklyn, Brooklyn. Home Sweet Home!"

Finally, through relentless negotiations, we decided to ask her to consider doing a two-week trial at the new place, and, after countless conversations and reasoning with her, she agreed. But just when we were ready to breathe a sigh of relief, she forgot she had committed to the trial and told us, "I never said I was doing a trial."

All through this time, I was running back and forth to my breast surgeon for scans, MRIs, or biopsies, and I was simultaneously being woken up in the middle of the night with my mother calling to tell me, "I'm not moving."

The day before her scheduled move-in day, my siblings made the final visit to her new apartment to drop off the last of her possessions. Everyone we spoke to, the staff, the social workers, the family of other residents, and countless articles on the internet said the same thing: It's really important that the new apartment feels just like her old home, so make sure you bring as many familiar items as possible. Accordingly, we moved her bedroom set, pictures, and her curio cabinet with her beloved Lladró figurines and a couple of other items into the unit.

That evening, Carl and I gently broached the subject of "the trial" move-in with my mom, and she exploded in a rageful rant. We had a terrible fight. We were all screaming at each other, which had never happened before, and this only subsided when Dan stepped in to say that he had heard enough. Thereafter, Carl and I distracted ourselves by cracking open a bottle of vodka.

Even with the vodka, I hardly slept that night. By 4:00 a.m., I got out of bed and started labeling the remainder of my mom's clothes, as we had been instructed by the facility to do this so that her laundry wouldn't get lost when sent out. I was also feeling guilty for snapping at my mother the night before, which was something I had never done before.

11

SHOWTIME

*A*t 11:00 a.m. the next morning, we told my mom it was time to go, and I fearfully thought she might refuse to get into the car. I didn't have a trick up my sleeve for getting her into the car, or for getting out of the car once we arrived at the assisted living facility. Luckily, she forgot that we said that she was going for "the trial" and thought she was going to visit the place to see if she liked it. I held my breath as we pulled up and she walked out of the car and into the building.

The staff eagerly awaited her arrival. The director of the facility, the nurse, the activity coordinator, and the social worker stood before her room, #232, with big smiles on their faces as we neared her door. The door had a big banner across it that read: *Welcome, Carmela*. The director handed my mom a pair of scissors, which, knowing what I knew, didn't seem like a great idea at the time. She asked my mom to cut the banner so she could enter the room.

Again, everyone was smiling. Among the team standing in

front of us, there was a combined experience of 90+ years working in the assisted living industry. My mom cut the banner and opened the door. She stepped inside and started screaming, "What did you do! What did you do!!! You took MY BED from my house and brought it here? Bring it back! I'M GOING HOME!!! HOME, HOME, HOME TO BROOKLYN, BROOKLYN, BROOKLYN!!!"

Everyone stared at each other and then looked at me and Carl. We looked at them as if they had some sort of magic spell to make this situation better. The director stepped in to try to appease my mom, but she was having none of that. She started walking toward the door and told me, "Rosemarie, let's GO. I want out of here NOW." I looked to the nurse with panicked eyes and whispered to her, "I have some Xanax in my purse. I could give her a pill."

The nurse replied, "You can't give someone a controlled substance that is not prescribed to them directly!" However, after about an hour of my mom's ranting with everyone trying to soothe and reason with her, the nurse leaned over and said to me, "Give her the Xanax—NOW!"

"I'm not staying here. Let's go. GET ME OUT OF HERE!" It was clear she wasn't getting any better. A doctor was called to prescribe some medication for her, and the social worker tried to reason with her. We called a companion service to come in to be with her 24/7, starting immediately, as the staff thought she might be a flight risk. I offered to sleep on her couch during the transition period, but the staff advised against it because seeing me was a reminder of her goal, which was to go back to Brooklyn. They preferred to have their staff work toward a successful transition. They were also aware of my health issues and wanted to protect me from any additional emotional burden.

This went on for weeks, with many sleepless nights and phone calls from my mother. I lost 10 lbs. in the two months prior to and during her move. Everyone in my close circle was extremely worried about me, but they didn't know there was still so much more to come.

12

1-800-FLUSHME

My BFFs Noreen, Maribel, Ann, and Lori came over to spend some time with me because they knew I was in a bad place. Dan was so happy that they were around so that he could tend to some bills and things around the house that had been put on hold. We started to talk about dieting. Noreen said, "I'm trying to limit my sugar intake. I was watching a video streaming on Facebook that said you can eat anything you want as long as it's in moderation."

"Duh, that doesn't sound like a gigantic revelation," Annie said.

"But listen to this," Noreen continued. "It said you can have Oreos every day as long as you creatively visualize and make a mental commitment, like a meditation, to only have two. So, I said 'I'm in!' I poured myself a glass of milk and took two Oreos out of the package. I dunked one, ate it, then dunked the other and ate it. There was only one problem."

"What's that, Noreen?" Lori asked.

"I had all of this milk left over."

"So, what did you do," Annie inquired.

"I ate the rest of the sleeve of Oreos. The problem was that I had too much milk!"

"What you needed was a shot glass of milk to accommodate your two Oreos," Maribel said.

"Dieting and exercise sucks, particularly after 50," I chimed in. "Yesterday, after I watched a Victoria's Secret commercial, I pulled out a lacy thong to put on because I thought it might make me feel better about myself since I've been in such a funk."

"That's good. Did it make you feel better?" Noreen asked.

"No. Worse," I said. "Instead of seeing a supermodel in the mirror, Yoshi the Sumo Wrestler was staring back at me! Even with the weight I've lost from the stress I'm under, it's Yoshi, not Gisele Bündchen, that I'm seeing."

Unbeknown to me, Lori had slipped away to go to the bathroom. She returned to inform me that my toilet was clogged.

I said to her and the other ladies, "You know, we've been having this problem for a couple of days now. I'm sorry. I should've told you guys to use the bathroom in the basement. I have a plumber coming tomorrow to fix the toilet."

The next afternoon, the doorbell rang, and I opened it to greet the plumber, a middle-aged man. "Thanks for coming," I said.

"My office told me you have a clogged toilet," he said.

"Yes, we've lived here 18 years, and this is the first time this has happened; my husband tried plunging a couple of times and can't fix it."

"Let's take a look," he said, and I escorted him to the bathroom with the problem. He took out his tools and removed the top off the commode to assess the problem. I told him I would be in the kitchen if he needed me.

As I busied myself around the kitchen, putting stuff away, I overheard the plumber say in a loud voice, "Jesus, Mary, and Joseph, there's sausages comin' out of this toilet! And meatballs too!" I rush into the bathroom. He paused and shook his head, looking directly at me and said, "Don't you people chew your food?"

My face turned beet red, and I said, "It's a long story. I'm Italian, and I love to cook," I stammered. "I've been in a rut lately, so I made a pot of sauce with meat last week, and I needed to throw some leftovers away. I flushed it down the toilet, maybe some stuff that I shouldn't have. But never mind that, can you fix it?" I pleaded with him.

"I'm going to have to take the whole toilet apart. You got some sausages stuck in the damn pipes. I ain't never seen anything like this in all of the 25 years I've been doing this!"

"Thank you!" I said. "While you're here, I'm just going to run to the supermarket to get a couple of things. I should be back in a half hour or so."

"I'll be here for a while." He shook his head again and mumbled to himself as he started taking the toilet apart. I got in my car as fast as I could to remove myself from the situation.

When I returned home, the plumber was on my front lawn, lifting up the entire toilet and shaking it. He was cursing and sputtering to himself. I looked at the clock, and it was a little after 3:00 p.m., and some of my neighbors were waiting outside to greet their kids coming off the school bus. As I hit the garage opener, I tried to look forward and scurry into the garage without having to interact with any of the neighbors.

But my neighbor Geri found me. She tapped on my

window, looking back and forth from the plumber to me and said, "Wow, that must have been some meal you made last night."

I shook my head and said, "Funny! Very funny!" I explained to her what happened.

Geri said, "My God, Ro, how much did you flush?"

"Nothing much," I mumbled. "Just four sausages and five meatballs."

"WHAT!?" she replied.

"Yep," my face was now red again.

"And you thought that nine pieces of meat were the equivalent of what might naturally go down the toilet?"

"OK, I get it. I fucked up. Dan's going to kill me when he finds out what I did. Especially when he sees this guy's bill!"

13

JANUARY 4TH, 2016

I can remember that moment as if it happened yesterday. I was sitting at my mom's assisted living facility, and it was the one-month anniversary of her moving in. The night before, I said to my husband, "You know, Dan, I'm finally feeling peaceful, starting to feel settled and alive again. I think this thing with my mom is going to work out, and I'm ready to start focusing on me and my upcoming radiation treatment. It's going to be OK."

My husband was my biggest supporter and champion. He kissed my hand and said, "You've been through a lot, but now you're turning a corner." I went to bed that night, and for the first time in a very long time, I fell asleep quickly and slept soundly.

The next day was a Monday, and I typically had a light workload at the beginning of the week. I finished up, did some errands, and decided to head over to see my mom for a while.

At 4:00 p.m., I found my mom sitting at her daily scheduled social hour at her new place, having a sing-along with the other residents, and, for the first time in a very long time, I smiled and said to myself, "This is nice. It's going to be alright."

At 4:01 p.m., my cell phone rang, and the genetic counselor from my hospital called to tell me that I tested positive for Chek2, a relatively new test.

Not one for small talk and a little blunt and to the point, she said, "Rosemarie, unfortunately this changes things significantly. By testing positive for the Chek2 genetic mutation, it makes you over 50 percent more likely to develop an invasive, stage breast cancer, and my recommendation is that you have a double mastectomy."

I stuttered and stammered some words back to her. Actually, I don't even remember what I said. I'm guessing that I thanked her for calling and letting me know. I returned to the table where, just moments ago, I happily watched my mom interacting with her new friends. My head was reeling, and panicky thoughts and feelings ran through my mind and body. I tried for a few minutes to pretend to be as happy as I was moments before. Then I jumped up from the table, made an excuse related to something that happened at work, kissed my mom goodbye, and placed an emergency call to my breast surgeon, who reaffirmed what the genetic counselor said. Fuck me, once again!

One step forward, one major step backward. I was now on the path to one of the most damaging, frightening journeys of my life. I would need to have my breasts removed.

I'm not sure how I drove home with all the tears flowing down my face at that moment. I called Dan and completely freaked out. He stayed on the phone with me until I was in the garage to make sure I made it back safely, and then he jumped into the car to head home from work to be by my side.

14

HELP ME!

I was so afraid. I felt like a caged animal trying to figure out how to get free. I wanted to run away and pretend the phone call and the doctor's confirmation of what needed to be done never happened. Now I had three LONG weeks to wait until the surgery. How did this happen? Who had ever heard of the Chek2 genetic mutation? When I shared that I tested positive for this, every doctor had to look it up on the computer to research what it was, as it had only been screened for the past five years, and they were mostly familiar with BRCA. To make matters worse, the genetic counselor shared that, of all the thousands of people screened by this lab, only .003 percent tested positive for Chek2. Oh wait, one more thing: The results also indicated that I had a possible chance of getting colon, kidney, or thyroid cancer, albeit with smaller odds than the breast cancer, but there was a chance, based on their findings. Four cancer genes, plus my previous lung cancer journey. Only *I* could win the Cancer Gene Lottery!

My brain was overloaded with panicky thoughts. I met with a reconstructive surgeon and started speaking with mastectomy patients from his practice. They answered my countless questions regarding the surgery, recovery, and restrictions. These led to more questions and more fear and anxiety. The most prevalent questions that kept cycling through my mind were: What if this cancer has spread through my body? How can I leave my kids and Dan now?

I was also terrified of having something so personal and intimate taken from me. It was a loss that was so different from something not visible to the human eye. Breasts, as well as extremities such as arms, legs, eyes, and hair, are part of what make up your physical appearance to others. Even though you don't show your breasts to others, there's still a significant difference between losing them versus having your gallbladder removed, especially as it relates to your sexuality, fear of lack of attractiveness to your life partner, or other things I had yet to process.

I was also afraid and mad at the interruption in my life. I know it sounds silly, but it was January and cold in the northeast, so this was the time my husband and I were going to take Latin salsa dance lessons because I wanted to know how to dance well with him. Additionally, I was mad that I was going to miss Super Bowl Sunday because it was only a week after my surgery—we were invited to a party, and I would not be well enough to go out by then. Plus, due to the surgery, I would have tubes and drains attached to me, and they would reside in a black fanny pack wrapped around my waist. I was more than positive that my showing up with a fanny pack filled with tubes under my button-down shirt would not go unnoticed—or perhaps gross people out as they tried to enjoy the Super Bowl.

The ironic part was that I didn't even like football, and I wasn't even remotely aware of who was playing, but I was upset that I couldn't sit in the kitchen with the ladies eating junk food and talking about normal, everyday things.

My doctor and some of his past patients told me about the restrictions and limitations I would incur following the surgery. I was so independent, not one to ask people to do things for me, but now I would have to ask people to open cabinets, lift things up for me, and drive me to various destinations. I had to stay home and recuperate, and I didn't want to have to do any of this, but I had no choice. A few people told me to enjoy my down time. REALLY? Having my breasts removed was down time, like taking a vacation? I was amazed at some of the stupid things people have said to me, mostly unintentionally, but nonetheless stupid.

I eventually stopped speaking, and I ate very little. Dan was concerned and asked me to say something, but I didn't have words to say, so I just cried. What cycled through my head was, "I can't do this! Why me? Wasn't lung cancer enough? I was just starting to get my mother settled and getting things back on track."

Speaking of my mother, she was still having a difficult time transitioning into the assisted living facility. Since I had been told that I couldn't visit her after the surgery for fear that I would pick up some sort of weird infection, like MRSA or C-Diff, I had been routinely visiting her now, and she was draining all my energy with her questions and demands, "I want to go home! When am I going home?" I finally decided to put myself before her, which was not something I usually do, especially with her. When she started with the questioning, I told her I just got a call from work and needed to leave. Self-care, something I was not used to doing, now seemed necessary when faced with situations such as this.

I did have an amazing support group, first starting with Dan, who was my rock—my soundboard for my darkest thoughts. It has been very hard on him to see me in this place and trying to get me through this. I overheard him telling someone recently that we had been to hell and back this year, with my health issues and my mother's exceedingly difficult transition to her assisted living facility. As best as I could, I was also trying to shelter my kids from this raw, emotional roller coaster I was going through, but they were 20 and 23 years old, so they were witnessing more than I would like them to see.

I spoke with my close circle of friends and family almost every night, and they listened to me cry, vent, and feel panic and hopeless. I felt bad that I was taking them away from their husbands and families, but I really needed them now. These were my "peeps," as I like to call them—they were always there for me, calling me and calling each other to figure out how to help me through this. My friend Loretta, who has been my friend since first grade, spent time on the phone with me every night, which I know is a sacrifice because she's married, and this took time from her evenings with her husband. But she knew how much I needed her now, along with my other friends, and I looked up to the sky and thanked God for these beautiful gifts I had been given, lifelong friends who rise up, and are there for me as I would be for them if they were faced with this difficult journey.

Another friend of mine since first grade, Rosemary, has been by my side, sending in food, visiting my mother because, this close to the surgical date, I had been forbidden by the staff at the assisted living facility to see her. She has been so warm and soothing. I was awestruck by the support I'd received.

15

MOM AGAIN

One of the hardest things was not having my mother by my side to care for and nurture me through this journey. As hard as it was, I decided not to tell her about my double mastectomy to protect her from knowing that her youngest child had cancer again—and that she must undergo yet another major surgery. My mom was well in 2008 when I had my lung surgery. She dropped everything in her life to take care of my children, my house, the cooking, the cleaning, and providing emotional support to me and my family. There was no love so profound and unconditional than a mother's, and my mother gave this to me when, at 44 years old, I had to have 10 percent of my lung removed. With her declining health and dementia, our roles had reversed. Her children were the parents, and she was the child. That was why I decided to shield her from this. I decided not to let her know what I was enduring because it would make her so distraught, agitated, and concerned, and I refused to let that happen!

Somehow with the support of my friends and family, especially Dan and the kids, I made it to the weekend before. My surgery was Monday, February 1st, and the hospital called me the Friday before to give me my presurgical instructions: No food or drinks after midnight the night before, I must be at the hospital at 7:00 a.m., I must wear a button-down top with no bra. They also told me more stuff that I wrote down and gave to Dan because it was too much to comprehend. The surgery would last six hours, and I would be in recovery for a minimum of one hour thereafter, then I would be brought to a private room.

I hung up the phone, shook my head, and thought to myself, "OK, Rosie, this is game time. You have to do this."

Directly after that, my friend Noreen called. I glanced at the clock, and it was 3:11 p.m., which was Marianne's birthday, March 11th, another indication that she was here with me today via one of her "winks from beyond." I shared the information that I'd just heard from the hospital with Noreen. She asked whether she and my other BFF Maribel could meet us at the hospital at 7:00 a.m. to be with me prior to the procedure. I told her that, yes, I would like that. As we were talking through what would occur on Monday, something struck me as being funny. I said to her, "I don't understand: Why is my surgery six hours long? My breasts are so tiny. I'm a small B-cup. I don't have gigantic boobs. You'd think my surgery would take half the time and be half the cost!"

Noreen responded, "That's funny! Also, you're fucked up!"

I AM fucked up. Only I would think of something like this.

16

THE NIGHT BEFORE

Sunday night, the night before the surgery, all my cousins got together with Dan and I, and we went out to dinner. I had a big bacon cheeseburger and fries because I felt I had earned it and would likely be eating very little after the surgery, so I wanted a treat. You could see from the look in their eyes how fearful my female cousins were for me. Surprisingly, after Dr. H, my reconstructive surgeon, drew the surgical markings on my breasts earlier in the evening—which was the sort of map of where he planned to make the incisions for the procedure—I finally felt a sense of permanence as to what would happen the next day. As best I could, I was ready for it. To lighten up the mood a little, I told my female cousins, "You know, I don't want to brag too much, but I just plucked my last nipple hair today." This, plus a couple of drinks, broke the ice and got us all to relax and enjoy the evening. We discussed plans for who would bring food in and help with laundry during my recovery. God bless my cousins, family, and friends for all that they did for us after my surgery.

Surprisingly, I slept the night before the surgery, woke up at 5:30 a.m., took what would be my last full body shower for quite some time, washed my breasts with the Hibiclens antiseptic soap, as instructed by the doctor, and I got dressed. I don't remember the car ride to the hospital, but I must say, for me, this was always the case — anticipatory anxiety was always worse than the actual event.

When I arrived at the hospital, I got undressed and casually spoke with my family and Noreen and Maribel. When the nurse came in to tell me they would be coming for me in 20 minutes, I noticed a dragonfly pendant on her shirt, and I knew that Marianne was by my side. Maribel and Noreen said they were leaving so I could have a few minutes alone with my immediate family. But, before they left, we did something spontaneous. We asked Dan and the boys to leave the cubicle. Then they drew the curtains closed, and I whipped out my breasts for them to say goodbye to them. We were like sisters, so we had seen each other's breasts before. Each of them jiggled my breasts. It felt cathartic to, for one brief moment, do something silly and funny during this serious time. It made us all smile. I then kissed my friends goodbye, and Dan and the boys came back in.

17

MARIANNE

This is what my son Greg wrote as his college entrance essay. He was overjoyed when he was accepted into his first-choice school. I found this essay shortly before my surgery. I thought about Marianne and what she meant to me, my children, and so many others. What was most significant about finding this just prior to my surgery was how she had been sending me her "winks from beyond," reassuring me along the way, especially since I was not quite sure what the outcome of my surgery and pathology report would be. Here is Greg's essay:

I wake up to the sound of my mom crying downstairs. Things are fuzzy to me as I try to shake myself out of the deep sleep I just left. I look at the clock—it reads 7:30 a.m.—and I struggle to leave my

dream world and enter reality. Suddenly, I remember what today is and why my mom is crying. Today is the day that we will say goodbye my mom's close friend, Marianne, who coincidentally is also my close friend Danny's mom.

It all started when two little boys moved to a block full of little girls. Our mothers formed an immediate friendship as they tried to navigate through the world of first-time motherhood and the raising of two very spirited little boys. Danny and I became close, lifelong friends, and brothers. We went to the park together, formed a weekly playgroup with other kids, had sleepovers as we got older, and basically did what all kids do. We were inseparable.

Although Marianne was ill with Crohn's disease, she did a great job hiding it, as she wanted to be as normal as possible. She volunteered her time and committed herself to becoming an activist for people less fortunate than herself. She spent endless hours helping others and finding ways to make a difference. Perhaps it was a distraction from her pain, but it was, nonetheless, a positive way to focus her energies.

When Marianne's cancer diagnosis came, it was a devastating blow to all the parents. Thinking back, Danny and I and the rest of the kids were too young to comprehend what it meant and what the consequences could be. They said it was intestinal cancer. It was hard enough for kids our age to wrap ourselves around cancer, let alone it being located in a place we didn't even know existed.

The one thing I remember learning from Marianne is how brave she faced her death. I was only 12 years old, but I can vividly recall how strong she was when she told her son she would be leaving him. I remember Danny telling me what she said, "One day, after I'm gone, you're going to be up in Gregory's room playing and you might suddenly feel sad because you miss me.

Maybe you'll hear Gregory's mom downstairs, and it will make you think of me. You need to know that I will always be with you. The difference is that I will be a part of you." This is something I have often thought about. As I grew older and was able to understand it better, it gave me comfort when I thought about the painful losses I may encounter in the future.

Marianne's funeral Mass was thus far the hardest and most meaningful day of my life. Perhaps the most moving part of the service was when we sat on the floor of St. B's Church and gathered around the guitarists as they played, and we sang Marianne's favorite songs— "Calling All Angels," "Drops of Jupiter," and most importantly, "Let It Be."

It still hurts me that my close friend was cheated out of all of this time with his mom. And I was cheated out of time with her as well. As I have grown older, I cannot help but question why some people's lives are cut short. Today I see the world through a new perspective. I look at how short life can be and all the things that Marianne has missed in her abridged life. Though I still haven't found the answer to why this happened to her, more importantly, I feel better prepared to face life's challenges head on and live life to its fullest.

Today I look at how this change in perspective has affected me. Because of Marianne, I have inherited her principle of the importance of helping others. I have volunteered at nursing homes, assisting the staff with the basic duties, and entertaining the elderly by merely listening to their life stories and playing music on the guitar for them. I have packaged and sent medication to those in need of basic nutrition in Honduras and founded a club at my high school that raised money for a shelter for homeless and abused children. I look at my past self, compared to the "me" now, to see *how evolved I have become and wonder, "Was this the turning point in my life?" "Have I become a better person after this?" I cannot be sure. What I am sure of is how truly proud of me Marianne must be. Thank you, Marianne, for all the lessons in life you have taught me. I love you.*

18

TODAY'S THE DAY

My double mastectomy took place on Monday, February 1st, 2016, at 9:00 a.m. It was performed by two doctors, my breast surgeon and a reconstructive surgeon, and the surgery lasted six hours.

The recommendation that I have a double mastectomy came three LONG weeks before the surgery, when the genetic testing results showed that I tested positive for the breast cancer gene. Prior to the genetic testing, I had had four biopsies, three lumpectomies, and a diagnosis of early stage cancer. When the doctors delivered the news that a double mastectomy was my best option, I cried, I screamed, I secretly made plans to ignore the results and run away to a tropical island, and I rocked back and forth in my bed at night holding my head in my hands telling my husband, "I can't do this."

Intellectually, I knew it was the right choice to make. By removing my breasts, I decreased my risk of developing an invasive "stage" cancer from over 50 percent to less than 1 percent.

That should be an easy decision, right? I couldn't wrap my head around making my way to the operating table and having my breasts removed. Instinctively, I knew that I would be changed by this. I can tell you with assurance that it DID change me. I know this to be true because when I had 10 percent of my lung removed in 2008 because I was diagnosed with Stage 1A lung cancer, I didn't feel different from anyone else. A double mastectomy was definitely way more personal.

So, I tried to figure out what I was going to do during the three weeks prior to the surgery. I looked within myself to see what I did in the past to soothe myself when faced with an uncomfortable, unknown situation. I remembered, when I was pregnant with my first child, I was nervous about becoming a new mom and worried how I would be able to handle having a baby. I did one of the classic things recommended in the pregnancy books: I nested. So, before my mastectomy, I decided to clean out the closets and the drawers, and I arranged everything in the kitchen and laundry room perfectly. Part of the reason for fixing up the kitchen and laundry room was that I knew that friends and family would be coming to help, and I didn't want them to really know how messy my house usually was. I journaled because many people told me that this would be therapeutic and helpful during this journey. I highly encourage this to anyone having to go through something life altering like this surgery so that you can look back when you hit your one-year anniversary to see where you were then and, hopefully, how much stronger you are now.

Another thing I did was earnestly think about and write down all the questions I had for both doctors, so, when I went for my presurgical visits, I had everything on paper. I woke up in the middle of the night to jot down something and even jumped out of the shower if questions came into my head if I thought I might forget them. I wanted to have all the answers, and I didn't want to have any surprises during the surgery and recovery period.

The night before the surgery, my husband and I met with Dr. H, my reconstructive surgeon, at his office at 5:30 p.m. so he could draw the surgical markings on my breasts. He took a Sharpie and drew the lines where he intended to make the incisions for the procedure the next day. For some reason, as I stood before him braless, he said to me, "You know, Rosemarie, for a 52-year-old woman, your breasts held up very nicely, no sagging; like a much younger woman."

To which I responded, "Thank you." Only when I left his office did I think to myself and say to Dan, "Well, what the hell am I going to do with that compliment; he's taking them off tomorrow, for God's sake!"

Surgery day. I must say that very few people saw and intimately knew the real me leading up to the day of surgery. To most people, including my coworkers, everyone admired how brave I was and how wonderfully I was handling the diagnosis and my reaction to the procedure. Countless people told me I was the strongest person they knew. That's the way I wanted it to be. This was a very personal experience, and I only let the people who could handle what was going on in my head know what I was feeling. This included the doctors. They marveled at how thorough I was in terms of the questions I had and how much I wanted to know prior to the procedure.

So, 15 minutes before the surgery, the breast surgeon popped her head into my presurgical cubicle where my family and two closest girlfriends waited beside me to ask if I had any last-minute questions. Everyone present knew how emotional I had really been and expected me to break down in tears with some last-minute panicked thoughts or questions. So, I said to the doctor, "I do have one question."

To which she responded, "Yes?"

I asked, "Can you play Billy Joel in the operating room?"

Everyone in the room burst into fits of laughter. You see, all my questions had been answered, except one. I remembered, during my pre-surgical visits, that the surgeon told me that she was as big a fan of Billy Joel as I am and had recently been to one of his sold-out concerts at Madison Square Garden. She told me long ago that she liked to play music in the operating room. I figured if I had to lie still for six hours I might as well enjoy some great music. She gave me the thumbs-up. I then kissed my husband and my sons, and off I went to the operating room with the hopes that Billy Joel was wrong when he sang, "Only the Good Die Young."—especially since Marianne was taken from us way too soon, and I was really hoping to stick around for a bit longer!

19

WHO KNEW?

*P*rior to the surgery, fear, panic, thoughts of running away—all these things flowed in and out of my head. But I also felt that the only way I could make it to the operating table was with the support of my close family and friends. Here was where things got a little tricky, and when I learned a valuable lesson that's worth sharing.

When people are scheduled for surgery, let's say an appendix, hysterectomy, even lung surgery, these are surgeries that no one can see after they're completed. Sure, you have scars, but they're covered by your clothing for the most part. However, having your breasts removed is a very personal experience and affects women on a different level than other surgeries. This loss can make you question your femininity, sexuality, attractiveness to your significant other, and a whole host of other things. It's hard to describe, unless you're actually in this space, how vulnerable and wounded you can be going into this surgery. Breasts are on the outside of our body, and even though they're also covered with clothes, they're something that people look at, ESPECIALLY when they know something is up with them!

I did not realize how important it was to be very careful with whom I shared my journey. Even more significantly, I should have made it crystal clear with them what my expectations were as they related to keeping this information private. Let me explain in greater detail: Upon learning that I was going to have a double mastectomy, I told my immediate family and some friends what was going on. My mistake was that I did not make it clear to anyone that they should not share this information with others. Because of that, many people that I'd rather not know were privy to what I assumed was confidential information. When you live in a suburban, close-knit community such as ours, news like this flies through town. Instead of being my personal journey, it became "this month's story." Everyone knew! I could have taken out a full-page ad in our local newspaper and less people would have known than had learned via word of mouth.

I felt wounded and betrayed that people I trusted with my story felt that they had the right to share it with others. That said, it was partly my fault because I didn't set boundaries by letting my people know that this information was for their ears only. I assumed that it was understood, but that was not the case. The net of this was that not only did so-and-so's friend know, but her husband knew, her kids knew, and this was very unsettling for me. If I could turn the clocks back, I would have done a better job in the communications department.

Chapter Takeaway: *If I had to give one piece of advice to someone about to embark on this or a similar journey, it would be that I encourage you to think long and hard about the circle of friends you share your story with, and, even more importantly, make it clear to them if you want to keep this information private and confidential. Moving forward, you'll avoid a lot of unsettling feelings and anxiety if you communicate your wishes clearly with your people. Physically, this journey is challenging enough. It will be easier emotionally if you're in control of and comfortable with who knows your story.*

20

FEBRUARY 1ST, 2016 – IT'S REALLY SHOWTIME

*H*ospitals must know that families get very emotional when the patient is being wheeled on the gurney down to the operating room and the family members follow along, so they trick them, probably for the best, by making them say goodbye to the patient halfway to the operating room near the door to the visitors waiting area. Dan cried, my kids cried, but surprising I did not. I kissed everyone and went into the operating room.

The operating room is a no-nonsense place. I've never been on the set of a movie, but it's what I envision might have a similar feel to it. Everyone has their job, and the timing is critical for doing it. The order in which things are done is imperative, and cues and directions are called out every step of the way. I only remember a little as I was knocked out soon after I arrived, but what I remember is the anesthesiologist saying, "OK, Rosemarie, on the count of three, we're going to need you to slide off the gurney onto this table. One, two, three." And off I went from one place to the next. They barked other instructions to me, which I, of course, obliged, and they called out additional necessary information for each other. The next and last thing I remember was someone strapping my arms down, which freaked me out a bit, and then I was out!

21

RECOVERY ROOM

When in recovery, I heard my name from time to time, "Rosemarie Mankes, moving to Room 272." I heard this as I faded in and out. I wasn't quite sure how I knew the timeline, because the nursing staff took away my glasses prior to the surgery, but I think it was from 3:00 to 4:30 p.m. At around 5:00 p.m., I think, I felt the gurney moving, and I knew we were on our way to our next destination. I distinctly remember Dan meeting us in the hallway, just before I entered the room. Even in my anesthesia haze, I remembered seeing so much love in his eyes, something I will remember, feel blessed to have, and appreciate for the rest of my life. They transferred me to the bed, and I tried as best as I could to settle in. My sons were there to take care of me, asking me what I needed or wanted every couple of minutes. I can tell you that **I WAS NEVER SO THIRSTY IN MY ENTIRE LIFE!** I guess after six hours of anesthesia, this might be a side effect that no one shared with us.

Noreen showed up and told Dan and the kids to go out to get a bite to eat, saying that she would take over. I think they were relieved to have a breather from a very stressful day. I must have asked Noreen every three minutes to please let me have some water. As the great, caring mother she was, she would put a straw in a cup of water, bend it, and bring it right to my mouth to drink. I gulped and gulped voraciously. And then again and again and again and again. I could not get enough of it.

After dinner, Dan sent the kids home to tend to what they needed to do, and he came back to relieve Noreen. Before she left, in my anesthesia, drug-induced haze, I asked for more water. Dan decided to take over, and, for whatever reason, he seemed to make it harder and harder, holding the straw farther from my mouth, making me struggle to reach it. This happened a couple of times before Noreen stepped in to show him how to do it.

It wasn't until a couple of months after the surgery that this memory popped up and Noreen said, "What the hell was up with Dan that night? He made you work so hard to get the straw to your mouth to get a drink."

I said, "You know, you're right. I don't know what was up, but if the circumstances were different, and it was his dick near my mouth, he would have had it front and center.

22

SLEEP TIME

Surprisingly, I didn't feel pain in my breasts following the surgery. The pain medicine ball the doctor had wired up to my breasts administered some sort of numbing meds, which were working like a charm. I had the morphine button next to me, which I was told I could push every time the light went on. I didn't feel it was necessary to do so, but Noreen said I needed to stay ahead of the pain, so every time it went off, she hit the button and subsequently knocked me into a coma. After a while, I told her to hold off on pushing the button, as the meds were starting to make me nauseous.

When it was time for bed, I told Dan to leave me a Xanax someplace that I could reach in case I woke up in the middle of the night and couldn't sleep. I'm sure administering your own meds in a hospital is illegal and unethical, but I really wasn't much into rules at that moment. Prior to the surgery, Dr. H had secured a private room for me and provided a bed next to me for Dan, so we tried to settle in for the night. Dan put his sleep apnea machine on and went off to sleep.

The nurse came in the middle of the night and scared the crap out of me as she began fumbling with the surgical dressings and checking my blood pressure, without bothering to whisper to me that she needed to assist me with this. After that, I was up, staring at the ceiling. An hour later, with no foreseeable sleep in my future, I decided to pop the Xanax. I reached into the place where I had hid it and tried to take it. Unfortunately, I dropped it. The pill was blue and oval. When I looked down at my hospital gown, ironically, the entire gown had little blue oval patterns on it. So, there I was in the middle of the night doing a treasure hunt on myself, trying to find the damn pill. After about 15 minutes of this unexpected mind-fuck game, I gave up and tried to quietly wake Dan up to have him give me another pill. However, his apnea machine was so loud that he couldn't hear me. Finally, I threw a water bottle at him, and he woke up to give me another pill.

At 6:00 a.m. the next morning, Dr. C arrived and woke me—but in a much nicer manner by gently rubbing my arm. She shared that everything went well. "As far as I can see, the breast tissue looked normal, no signs of tumors or anything that might indicate a more aggressive cancer. But, given the positive results of the genetic testing, I think you made the right decision."

"Thank God," I replied. I asked her some questions as to what the next steps were, when I would be going home and some other things that I don't really remember. She answered them, but I noticed that she kept looking over curiously at Dan.

Being in sales for years and keenly aware of body language, I realized what she was thinking as she looked at Dan with the apnea machine on. I said, "I know. He looks like someone on life support and more like the patient than I do." We both laughed, and Dan slept through the entire encounter.

23

THE DRAINS

"Physically, the worst part is the drains." Not the pain of having your breasts removed, not the limited mobility, not losing your ability to drive. "The worst part is the drains." That's what five former mastectomy patients told me before I had the surgery.

Prior to my surgery, I was terrified about having my breasts removed. I wasn't really worried about pain because I have a pretty high tolerance for pain. After all, when I had my lung surgery in 2008, the surgeon had to spread and crack my ribs to make his way to my lung; that was pretty painful, and I soldiered through that journey. Before my mastectomy, I was more afraid and pretty angry about having my life interrupted and becoming dependent on others to do simple, mundane tasks like reaching up into my kitchen cabinet for a coffee cup, or showering, or washing my own hair, or being able to cook for my family or DRIVE. Having to forgo driving for four to six weeks was a big sacrifice, and, even more so, having to ask family and friends to take me from here to there was very unsettling for me.

Even still, somehow, I adjusted to those things. The real tipping point was when I was informed that I would be coming home from the hospital after the mastectomy with the drains. By definition, the drains are four tubes connected to the lower part of my breasts (two on each side) that would be capturing breast fluid in little containers, referred to as bulb syringes. These bulbs would reside in a fanny pack wrapped around my waist. I was terrified when told that my husband and I would have to empty the fluid from the bulbs three times a day, measure the amount, and report back to the doctor's office. Not being medically inclined and more than a little squeamish, I became weak in the knees and filled with worry about looking at and handling this breast fluid on a daily basis. I was obsessed and worried that the fluid might smell or leak onto my clothes.

For some out there, this may not be a big issue if you've been through this journey. For me, it became a hugely contentious matter because my drains were overachievers and produced an enormous amount of this fluid every day. After a couple of days, I needed to find levity in the situation and started calling this awful fluid "breast juices." I was told that, on average, it takes 10–14 days for the drains to come out, but the staff at my practice said that my drains would probably come out sooner because I was thin and fit. After my mastectomy, my drains were still putting out lots of breast juices — 16 LONG days' worth — with no end in sight! Finally, the surgeon said that they had to come out, or I risked getting an infection. During my reconstruction surgery, I was once again overflowing with breast juices, and, 15 days in, I was ready to yank them out myself. Thankfully, they were removed on day 16 once again!

I couldn't understand it. It's not like I had these enormous breasts prior to surgery. I was a small B-cup at best. Where was all this fluid coming from? Puzzling! Another problem with having the drains is that you have to walk around with a fanny pack every day, carrying the bulbs that collect the fluid. This fanny pack wraps around your waist and sometimes the pack dips low. After a couple of days of the bag dangling down near my crotch area, my sons started to say I looked "gangsta," and they called the bag "my balls." I became accustomed to adjusting the bag every time I sat or stood up, so I guess the assessment was pretty accurate.

Thankfully, I have a wonderful group of friends and family, and they sent food in or came over to cook for my family. During this time, I also had frequent visitors, who distracted me from these awful drains and how uncomfortable they are. They helped alleviate my depression about not being able to leave the house. I'm very thankful for how everyone I love mobilized and was with me during this, one of the most challenging times of my life. God bless my peeps!

Chapter Takeaway: I'm not sure there was a lesson or "Aha!" moment here except to say that the drains were limiting and challenging, but they were also temporary. I drove myself nuts counting the days and having unrealistic expectations that, somehow, I would get them out sooner than later. They came out when my breast juices were ready to stop flowing. I did not have control over that. What I should have done was binge-watch Netflix.

24

SETTLING IN

I was sitting on the couch, watching an episode of *Ray Donovan* with Dan, when my husband said, "How's your pain level on a scale of 1 to 10?" I responded, "It's a 5, not strong enough to take the painkillers." I had been home for two days now, following my mastectomy.

The phone rang, and it was my mom. "Rosemarie, I don't know how or why I'm in this place, but I'm not staying. Make sure you come here tomorrow morning with a truck and bring all of my stuff back to Brooklyn!" I handed the phone to Dan because I didn't have the strength to take this on tonight. He spent some time reminding her that she was staying at the place on a trial basis and had the ability to leave after the trial was over.

I headed upstairs to my bedroom because I had to remove myself from this situation. I'd been down this road over and over and my mom's transition had been taking a toll on me emotionally. Based on her declining health and progression of her dementia, she needed to be in an assisted living facility. I reminded myself that she was now safe, healthy, and receiving good treatment.

I decided that I had to do a little self-care as it related to my mom. I would continue to visit her when I get clearance from my doctors, but, when the conversation turns into a battle, even if it's after just a few minutes, I would pick up, make a work-related excuse, and leave.

It was difficult wrapping myself around this cancer journey, the unknowns, the what if's—especially if they find something indicating a more invasive cancer within the pathology report.

On a lighter note, the life coach course materials arrived today, and, as soon as I felt strong enough to crack open the books, I would email my mentor, Michele, to let her know I was ready to start the training. I was excited that I would soon be able to help others experiencing difficult hurdles, similar to what I've had to face.

25

RESULTS

Dr. C called today with great news. The pathology report came in: all margins were clean, and I was cancer free. I began to cry and say, "Thank God, Thank God, and Thank you!"

"Rosemarie," Dr. C continued. "We did see a radial scar within the tissue samples, which never showed up in any of your imaging and screenings. In my experience, when a radial scar presents itself in breast tissue, it can turn into an invasive cancer. I truly believe you made the right choice in having the double mastectomy."

As I thanked her again, I looked up at the sky and thanked God and my guardian angels for this blessing. I'd been wearing a bracelet every day since my surgery, and it read, *She believed she could, so she did,* and today I felt the truth in those words. I hung up the phone to call Dan and the kids to tell them the good news. Through lung and breast cancer, someone wants me to stick around! My plan was to do something meaningful with the things I have learned in my life, which has been filled with curveballs, and I was now ready to take it on. I was just waiting for the right time to do so.

26

WHAT A CLUSTER-FUCK!

A couple of weeks after my surgery, one of my close friends called me to see how I was feeling. "How are you, my friend?" she asked.

"Physically, I'm doing well," I responded. "Emotionally is another story." I went on to explain that, besides feeling upset about the whole surgery thing, I was feeling that there were a couple of people in my life who were causing anxiety, and, after a lot of careful consideration, I wanted to move away from them. There was one person in particular I felt strongly about cutting ties with.

My friend replied, "You know that my mother is very spiritual and knows a lot about these things. I'm going to tell you what she taught me to do when you have someone bringing negative, toxic energy to you and you need to get rid of them."

I was all ears.

"Here's what you do. You go to a store and buy a doll, like a

Barbie Doll and some honey. Then you come home and fill a glass halfway up with the honey and then you put the doll in the glass face down with its face turned away from you, like the doll is facing the outside of your house. For some reason, this person will then get the message that you don't want to be associated with them, and they will move away from you so that you can end the relationship."

Weird as it sounded, I was all over this. The next day, Dan and I went to the store, and I bought what my friend had told me to get. We came home, and I started following the instructions verbatim.

Coincidentally, my friend called to check in on me. "What's up," she said.

"It's so funny that you called," I replied. "I was just pouring the honey into the glass when the phone rang, and I just put the doll in face down, facing away from me. How crazy is it that you called now!"

"Hang on one minute, my mother is on the other line," my friend said. So, for the next two minutes, I listened to my friend speaking back and forth to her mother on the other line in Spanish. Then I heard her say, "Ay dios mio!" and I knew something was wrong.

She hung up with her mom and started shouting, "I got the formula wrong! Oh my God, Oh my God. Putting the doll in honey is what you do when you want to sweeten a relationship with someone, not get rid of them. Get the doll out of the honey and throw the doll and the cup away. THROW BOTH AWAY!!! If you keep it in the honey, the person you're trying to get rid of will be all over you like flies on shit! You'll never get rid of them!"

So, there I was, like an idiot, yanking the doll out of the cup and throwing both away. I started sweating profusely and said, "What the fuck, so what am I supposed to do now?"

My friend said, "My mom just told me that the way to get rid of a toxic person is that you have to write their name on a piece of paper—their full name. Then you get a small container, like Tupperware, and fill it halfway with water. You take this person's name and put it face down in the water, seal the container, and put it in the freezer. **That's the way to get rid of someone. You have to freeze them, and then they will move on and be out of your life.**" So that's what I did. I wrote out the full name, got out a container that I knew I wouldn't need. Then I filled it with water, put the paper upside down, and froze this person. I'm not sure if it's a coincidence or what, but it worked. Little by little, the person started to move away from me, called less, and eventually not at all.

About a year later, we lost power in our house, and everything in our freezer defrosted. There was this person's name floating around in the container in the freezer. Sure enough, the person tried to reach out to me to try to rekindle the relationship. I gave some vague excuse as to why I wasn't available and immediately refroze the paper when the power went back on. Thus far, things have been quiet, and I think I have successfully transitioned away from this person.

27

THE POSITANO

16 steps up, 16 steps down – that counted as one flight...

About a month and a half after my mastectomy, I was beginning to become a little antsy, feeling the need to burn off some energy. I called my doctor's office, and they said that my exercise restrictions were still in place. The only thing I was cleared to do was walk. Since it was mid-March in New Jersey, which is freezing, and I hate the treadmill, this did not leave me with many options, so I decided to create my own exercise regimen. I called it, "The Positano."

During the three times we visited Italy, we stayed in the magical town of Positano, which is utterly beautiful and rich with exciting Mediterranean views. Anyone I know who has visited has always been delighted and mesmerized by the homes, villas, and hotels built into the mountain and overlooking the sea. However, one thing to know about Positano is that the only way to travel up and down the mountain by foot is to walk hundreds and hundreds of steps up and then down.

The people who live in this village have legs that are extremely muscular and toned because it's the only life they've ever known.

One day, while recovering from my mastectomy, I was feeling pretty anxious and sad about not being able to work out in the way that I liked. I decided to utilize my energy by walking up and down my home steps several times a day—16 steps up and 16 steps down, then again and again—to help me burn off some steam. It took me some time, but, after a month or so, I was doing 75 complete flights, or the equivalent of approximately 2,500 steps per day. After this, my endorphins started coming back, and I was starting to feel stronger and more alive. I did this for several months after my mastectomy and then again after my reconstructive surgery as it kept me sane and active and helped me push through the tremendous energy, anxiety, and need to keep moving during this journey.

Chapter Takeaway: When faced with difficult challenges, where you might experience disruptions or limitations related to your usual workout routine, improvise, if possible, and create a new exercise regimen. That's how the Positano was born!

28

WHO'S LOOKING AT YOU?

The drains were out. I had clearance to drive, and I was starting to feel a bit more normal, so Dan and I headed out for the first time to a social event.

But, when the lady with the sultry voice on the navigation system in our car announced that we would arrive at our final destination in five minutes, suddenly and quite unexpectedly, my heart started to pound, and I began to sweat. I silently tried to calm myself down, but, after a minute or two of trying, I turned to my husband and said, "Dan, I'm not sure if I can do this." The urgency in my voice took him aback. He pulled the car over to the side of the road.

Today should have been a happy day. Today, my husband and I were attending the wedding of one of my closest friends' sons. It would likely be a wonderful party, with lots of good food, wine, and dancing. However, for me, it was also the first time I was attending a fancy social event following my double mastectomy. It was the first time that I was getting dressed up in big girl clothes with high heels to head out for a night on the town. Sounded like fun, didn't it?

When I accepted the invitation, and through the months leading up to the wedding, I was excited to have something to look forward to. After all, for close to two months, I was restricted by my surgery and the down time for healing. What I didn't realize was that this was one of the first times that people —not close friends—but other people were going to see me after my surgery. One thing I knew for certain was that things had changed as a result of my surgery. Let me explain. Prior to having a double mastectomy and before anything ever happened with my breasts, people looked into my eyes when they met me. Since then, people have started looking down at my breasts first and then looking up. Some may think I'm being overly sensitive or paranoid, but I'm not. Trust me, as a small B-cup prior to my surgery, my breasts were not something anyone was interested in taking a peek at. But now they were, and that makes me feel uncomfortable and different than I was before. I worried that I would see a sorrowful look in their eyes or, worse yet, feel pitied by these people.

As we sat on the side of the road, I told Dan I didn't want to go to the party. However, this clearly wasn't an option since it would be terribly disappointing to my friend Bonnie—and to me as well. After a brief but intense discussion, off we went. We arrived at the venue. The valet guy opened my car door, and out I went on shaky legs into the hall. I immediately grabbed a glass of champagne, which calmed me down somewhat.

The anxiety I was feeling totally knocked me off balance. I'm not normally a socially anxious person; I LOVE a good party. I tried to look at myself introspectively to see what was happening and how I could soldier through these feelings and the wedding for that matter. I asked myself, "What are you afraid of? Why are you worried about the people who are attending, who will be sitting with you at the reception, and what they might think when they see you?" Frankly, the only people I really knew and were close to were the immediate family of the groom. The others were merely acquaintances at best.

I reasoned with myself saying things like, "You're a guest at this party. You're not the mother of the groom. All eyes are not going to be on you!" Still I was unsettled, but with a lot of self-talk and deep breathing, I made it through the ceremony and headed to the cocktail hour.

That's when I realized I needed to identify the people I was afraid to see at our assigned table at the reception, visualize the encounter in my mind, sort of role-play it, and map out how I would react to it. These are some of the many tools I'm learning from the life coach training.

So, that was what I did during the cocktail hour. I identified the women and their husbands I was worried about seeing, and I visualized their sideway glance downward when they saw me and what I thought they might be thinking as they looked at me. I decided that they were inconsequential, and I should not care what they did or thought. After lots and lots of self-talk, role-playing, and visualization, again via the life coach training, and it was time to head into the reception.

Exactly what I thought and feared would happen occurred. We arrived at our assigned table, and, sure enough, I was greeted by these people in the way I thought I would be—not by all of them, but some of them. They looked down, which gave me that vulnerable, "I am different feeling," and then they looked up. But it was OK because I anticipated what would happen beforehand and rehearsed it, so to speak. By doing this work, it kind of took the steam out of the kettle or the helium out of the balloon. It happened, and it was over.

But the story doesn't end here. While making my way across the room to congratulate my friend on her son's wedding, a woman—a total stranger—walked up to me and said, "I just have to tell you, I'm on the board of directors for the top fashion design school in New York City, and I must say that by far you're the best dressed woman here. You carry the look so well." You can only imagine how fast my jaw dropped to the ground. Whoa, I did NOT see that one coming! I couldn't believe it. I briefly told her the background of the earlier story, hugged her, and thanked her for being there for me tonight.

I did encounter similar social anxiety three more times at other events after the wedding, but I knew there was a chance that this might occur, and I was able to use the new skills I was being taught from the coursework I was learning. I was better prepared for the feelings and, as a result, they were not as hard to deal with. As for the original wedding, we danced, we ate, and we drank at the reception, but, most importantly, we celebrated a beautiful milestone with our dear friends.

On the way home from the wedding, Dan said he needed to go to the bathroom, so we got off at the next rest stop exit. I figured I might as well go too, as the drive home was going to be at least an hour, without traffic. When I entered the ladies room stall, this is the sign I saw on the door facing me:

> Please Help Keep This Restroom Clean
> Do Not Pee on the Floor
> No Drawing on the Walls
> Do Not Spit on the Floor or in the Sink

This Is Your Bathroom!

I shook my head and took a photo of it, saying to myself and to Dan shortly thereafter, "What kind of women have they encountered that would require them to make up this sign? How many women pee or spit on the floor or in the sink? You just can't make this shit up!"

Chapter Takeaway: If you're feeling social anxiety regarding an upcoming meeting, event, or situation, try role-playing and visualization prior to the event as a way to better prepare yourself for it.

29

DIMES

I have a confession to make. For quite some time, I have been putting a dime in my left shoe heads up every day. Even *I*, someone who is a bit out there these days, would think this is strange. But something interesting happened to me just at the point that I finished the coursework and was about to start developing my plan to work as a life coach. This occurrence made it imperative I carry a dime on me every day.

I was feeling apprehensive about starting as a life coach. I was very interested in working with women who were diagnosed or going through the breast cancer journey, but I felt apprehensive as my situation was still so new. I questioned whether I would be able to provide value at this stage in my journey. I had a big meeting scheduled the next day with the owner and office manager at a large breast imaging center, and I, Rosie Mankes, had to prove to them and myself that I could join their life coaching team as a consultant for patients who were interested in my services.

Switching gears completely for a moment, know that I'm not a person who carries loose change on me. If I pay cash for something, which is rare as I usually use my credit card to get mileage, I throw the change into my cupholder in my car.

The morning before the appointment, I went into my closet to pick out a pair of pants to wear. As I pulled them off the shelf to put them on, four dimes came out of nowhere and bounced on the shelf in front of me—clink, clink, clink, clink. I can tell you with assurance that they did not come out of the pants pockets, as I wore these pants the day before and there was definitely no exchange of currency.

This made me curious, so I Googled the meaning of finding dimes, and a couple of sites said that *"Finding dimes is guidance or validation from your guardian angels that you're on the right path."* I put the dimes in a cup and headed to work for the day.

That evening, I was still stressed about the meeting the next day, so Dan suggested we take a walk by the ocean, as he knew that this was soothing to me. It was fairly late in the evening, so there were very few people out and about. As Dan paid for parking at the parking meter, a dime rolled past my foot like a bike tire would roll by if a person was riding past me. I picked up the dime, shook my head, and said to Dan, "That makes five dimes for today."

After the walk and while driving home, I decided that my dimes deserved a special place in my home since someone, and I suspect it might be Marianne, was trying to tell me something about my new pathway into life coaching and motivational speaking. I picked out a pretty, ornate container to put my dimes in and headed upstairs to put them on my nightstand next to my bed. When I got there, I was amazed at what I saw. There was a dime sitting on my nightstand.

I have lived in my house for almost 19 years, and I, like most women, know exactly what I have on my nightstand . . . whether it be hand lotion, tissues, a candle, medicine, whatever. There was never a dime on my nightstand, but there was one sitting on my nightstand that evening. Six dimes in one day!

I put my dimes in the special container, went to bed, and headed to the appointment the next day, knowing that there was a reason that I was doing what I was doing, that I was meant to do it and make a difference and impact in other people's lives.

Some may wonder, why do I put the dime in my left shoe? First, I'm left-handed, so that seemed like a natural fit. Second, I knew that the dime needed to be close to my body and having it in my purse seemed too far away. I originally started by carrying the dime in my back pocket, as the pants I wear do not have front pockets, but I have a habit of putting my phone in my back pocket. After losing a couple of dimes when I inadvertently pulled my phone out, and the dime fell out without me knowing, I had to make a choice as to where the dime went. So, here were my options: in my bra, in my panties, or in my shoe. I went with the left shoe as that seemed the least weird of the three!

The dime is a constant reminder of what I intend to do. It's like having a rock in your shoe, nagging at you as you walk. But, for me, it's just what I need. I feel it there, and it tells me to stay focused and keep moving forward with my plan. I ended up having a great meeting with the owner and office manager of the breast imaging center. We put my cards out in the waiting area, and shortly thereafter I started receiving calls and seeing new clients.

30

RECONSTRUCTION

The time had finally come for me to have the reconstructive surgery, where my surgeon would swap the expanders and replace them with the implants. I was smart enough to know that this was part of the journey. However, I hadn't processed this within my head properly. Having the reconstructive surgery would also mean I would incur a major setback physically, and I would need to return to having the restrictions, relying on others, and having to deal with the damn drains as I had before. This put me into a depressed place for a bit of time.

Some may read this and think I should be happy that I was getting my new breasts, but I have always been someone who lives for today and does not like—even deplores—downtime, particularly when it makes me feel weak and dependent. This additional interruption in my life was hard for me to swallow. Plus, I didn't want this at all. I was happy with my tiny breasts and would never have gone out of my way for implants, except, in this particular circumstance, to save my life.

That meant another three-hour surgery, oodles of anesthesia, and time to recover—with the God-forsaken restrictions. Three days after the procedure, the anesthesiologist called to see how I was feeling. I thought this was odd because I would think he'd reach out the day after. I told him I was fine and that I have been keeping my diet light because, in the past, I had gotten sick from anesthesia. He said, "I wouldn't worry about eating; from what I could see during the day of the surgery, your body looks beach ready to me!"

Not thinking clearly, I said, "Oh, thank you." He gave me his cell phone number and told me to call him if I needed anything at all. After I hung up and processed the conversation, I realized that he had only seen me naked on the operating table. I thought to myself, *This guy is creepy!*

Later that evening, a couple of my friends, Noreen, Maribel, Annie, Geri, and Lori came over to spend some time with me. They brought wine and some light snacks, and I allowed myself to have my first glass of wine since the procedure. Because I wasn't taking any of the pain meds, I thought it would be OK to indulge, just a little. As Maribel poured the wine, she and my friends made a toast to me and my health, and we clinked glasses. Mine broke as I tapped it against theirs. There was wine all over the table, and the girls quickly jumped up to clean it up. I immediately reminisced about that time, so long ago, when Marianne shared that breaking a glass was a sign that she was with us. Tears streamed down my face as I looked up to the sky and said, "Thank you for being by my side!"

31

ROAD TRIP

A couple of weeks after the reconstructive surgery, Dan knew I was feeling a little down and out and suggested we take a drive to IKEA to pick up some furniture for one of the boys' apartments. To get outside of my head, I agreed to go.

Let me tell you something about IKEA: You could make it through the Vatican, viewing all the exhibits, three times before you could find your way out of IKEA. You enter IKEA via an escalator, and then you're enveloped by this all-consuming maze that forces you to view every item and every room in-store, yet you still can't get out. After we found what we wanted, we started to exert tremendous mental energy in trying to find the checkout counter so we could leave. We kept seeing one EXIT sign after another, which led us to yet again another room we hadn't visited. Finally, when we thought we might have seen it all, we saw a sign that said "check out." We excitedly pushed our way through the sea of other confused customers, only to find ourselves in the food court.

But this wasn't your run-of-the-mill food court with burgers, fries, and churros. They were serving salmon, Swedish meatballs, and a variety of kale salads. People were sitting there eating like they were dining at a fine restaurant in Manhattan. Jokingly, I said to Dan, "You want to take me to IKEA for dinner next Saturday night?" which would never happen because I don't plan to ever go back there in this lifetime if I can help it. Not to mention, IKEA for dinner on a Saturday night? I don't think so.

Last observation about IKEA: I think they have some sick, twisted, demented employee who comes in the middle of the night and screws with the wheels on the carts because there was not one customer in the store who could wheel their cart in a straight, linear line. Every single one of us was zig-zagging through the store just like when you get the bum cart at the supermarket. After you finish shopping, you've worked so hard navigating the cart that you think you might need a hip replacement. Zigging and zagging through IKEA made our quest to get out even more difficult. At one point, I turned to Dan and said, "You need to take over wheeling the cart because, if I keep pushing, my boobs are going to dislodge and end up on my back!"

Somehow, we made it out, and I needed to take a nap when we returned home.

32

WHAT ARE FAMILY AND FRIENDS?

They're the people who rush off the other line when I call because they know I need to talk or cry, and they're there to listen or comfort.

They're the people who go to the store, juggle my schedule, and continue to run my life smoothly when I don't have the time or strength to do so myself.

They're the people who cancel their own plans so they can take me where I need to go because they know I cannot drive myself.

They're the people who cook for my family or send in food because, based on my current situation, I'm incapable of putting a meal on the table myself.

They're the people who help me heal by creating new memories between us in the years ahead.

I'm honored to have you in my life.

I love you.

33

MOM AGAIN

My mother had been in the assisted living facility near my house for four months now. She has weekly visits with a social worker, and the nurses reported she was finally starting to settle in. She still called or told me during visits that she wanted to go back to Brooklyn, but this had become our new normal, so I just answered by saying, "I'm really tired today; can we talk about this tomorrow?" Somehow, this would always appease her, and we could go on to another conversation for a couple of minutes until she forgot and asked again. I found it easier, during my visits with her, to steer the conversation into the past, like the 1950s and 1960s, and ask questions about her siblings, parents, cooking, and her life back then. Her memory was laser sharp when it came to this time in her life, but it was shot when it came to short-term memory. That was the devastating thing about dementia; you watch the person you know and love slip away from you, not physically but mentally, right before your eyes. And it SUCKS!

A new resident named Anna moved in last month. My mom and her quickly became close friends and formed a little circle of ladies who hang out together. Then the best thing that could happen occurred. They started a poker game, which takes place three times a week. My mother LOVES gambling, especially poker, and suddenly my mom was asking less and less often when she was going home.

Last week was exceedingly busy at work for me. I tried as hard as I could to get to see her each day, and now it was Friday, and I was finally able to make it over there. I was feeling guilty, as I usually went for a visit at least twice a week. When I arrived at 4:00 p.m., the residents weren't gathered around the table for their normal social hour, so I asked the receptionist where they might be.

"Oh," she said, "they're all upstairs in the activity room playing blackjack. The facility brought in a professional blackjack dealer today as one of their activities."

"Hmm," I said to myself, "I'm home working all day feeling guilty that I'm not here, and she's playing blackjack. Rosie, you need to stop torturing yourself. She's doing fine!"

I went upstairs to see her, kissed her hello, and sat for a while watching the residents play. My mom had a big smile on her face, particularly since she was winning. After about 45 minutes, she leaned over and whispered in my ear, "Rosemarie, when am I getting out of here? I want to go back to Brooklyn!"

I said, "Enjoy your game. We'll talk about it tomorrow." Deflection, just like when my children were young. That's what I do now because I must detach myself to make it through. As I made my way out of my mother's place, I glanced over at the front desk and saw a bouquet of sunflowers sitting on the counter. They were Marianne's favorite flowers—and just the reminder I needed to feel her presence. Even though it felt shitty to leave my mother mid-way through the visit, my friend was telling me it was OK to take care of myself and leaving as I just did was the best option for me.

34

LOSS

I missed my nipples. They were the way to get the party started when my husband and I made love, and sometimes they were what helped me get to the finish line when other things weren't working. Some of my mastectomy friends told me that we would need to explore other erogenous zones to replace my nipples. For the past year, we have been doing just that. I know that it turns me on when my husband kisses the back of my neck, but one of my favorite sexual positions is to be on top, facing him, so unless I can channel Linda Blair from *the Exorcist* and rotate my head backwards in our bedroom, I'm not quite sure how I can use this one to get to the finish line. TMI, I know, TMI.

But that was not the only reason I missed my nipples. For me, personally, nipples were like sprinkles or chocolate syrup on ice cream. They belonged together and complemented each other. Everyone is different, but I felt that nipples belonged on my body. I think I would look in the mirror, after they return, and feel just a little more complete. They would camouflage the incision lines that run horizontally through the center of each of my breasts, and, if they look anything like the 3-D tattoo photos I've seen, I'll be happy to close this chapter in my life and move on.

Some people are fortunate to have nipple-sparing mastectomies. Since most of my cancer was right behind my nipples, my doctors thought it was best that we do not try to save them, as there could potentially be some errant cancer cell that might be embedded in my nipples. So off they went with both of my breasts on February 1st, 2016.

There were many options, regarding new nipples—reconstructed nipples, tattoos, and many women choose to forgo them altogether. This is a very personal and individual decision. I chose to go to a famous 3-D nipple tattoo artist named Vinnie in Maryland to have my nipples created on May 3rd. To my surprise, the procedure required only one visit, and it lasted just one hour.

So, now I had to choose the size and shape of my nipples. My goal was to make them look similar in pigment and size to my original ones because I liked them. Prior to the procedure, a few of my BFFs would come to my house, and we would look at photos on Vinnie's website to earmark the ones we thought looked best. Fortunately, I had a few photos of my original breasts that we could compare them to. Once we narrowed it down to the top three pairs, I presented them to my husband for him to weigh in on. After all, it was only he and I who were going to see them on a regular basis, and he needed to be happy with this decision.

Recently, my two sons were home for the weekend having breakfast with us. With one working and living in New York

City and the other away at college, it was very rare that we all had time to sit down together at home for a meal these days. One of my sons had his shirt off, and I began looking at his bare chest. Both of my children are fortunate to have my husband's physique—muscular, well-built chests and body frames. But, strangely enough, on this day, I was not looking at my son and admiring how handsome he was; I was fixated on his nipples. I decided that his were too small, so I asked my other son if I could see his chest. Not knowing where I was going with this, he pulled his tank top up to show me and Ding, Ding, Ding! We had a winner. My other son had the right size nipples, with the right pigment. I asked him if I could take a picture of his nipples to bring to Vinnie. Of course, this did not go over well with my 20-something-year-old child.

His face turned beet red, and he said to me, "Are you crazy? You want to bring a picture of my nipples to the mastectomy tattoo guy? Do you think I have nipples that look like a woman's?"

OK, so maybe that idea was a little too out there, and I needed to stick with the original plan with my girlfriends.

Back to my friends, they were actually a little insulted that they were not invited to come when I had my nipples put on. I think that they secretly wanted to be in the room when Vinnie did his work, but that was where I draw the line. My husband could be in the room with Vinnie and me, but that was it. I didn't want the procedure recorded or any spectators besides Dan. I mean, for God's sake, would you want your BFFs in the room with you when you slide down with your legs in the stirrups to get your annual PAP smear?

I saw a segment done by Joan Lunden on *the Today Show* featuring women going to Vinnie to get their nipples tattooed after undergoing mastectomies. Through the years and thousands of tattoos Vinnie has created for women, a catchphrase was born when the procedure is done, and he has completed his work: "I got Vinnied." So, on May 3rd, Rosie Mankes would happily join this group and "Get Vinnied!"

35

WHO AM I?

When I was a young adult, I believed I was super ambitious. I set goals for myself and accelerated the timeline for doing them. I was voted Most Likely to Succeed in elementary school, and I graduated high school and then college in three vs. four years, completing my education in 1984. Why? I couldn't explain it now as a woman in my fifties, but, at the time, I thought that it would escalate my career and the success that I expected in life. The first line of the song "Vienna" from Billy Joel comes to mind when I reminisce about that time: "Slow down, you crazy child; you're so ambitious for a juvenile." That was me!

For a little while, when I was working in advertising sales for magazines, I was extremely successful and highly sought after. I felt it, that *high* that you feel when you're respected in the workforce, your opinion matters, and you command attention! I was the top producer in my office. Publishers of the bestselling magazines tried to pull me away from my current job with very attractive, lucrative offers. The senior VP/publisher of the very last job I worked at told me several years after I left the industry, and after she had worked with countless ad sales professionals, that I was by far the best one she had ever worked with—a powerful comment that made me feel alive and validated.

In 1995, when my youngest son Jordan was born and came home from the hospital with a heart apnea monitor because he could potentially be a SIDs baby, our nanny fell apart when we all went for CPR training; it was too stressful for her to handle. She was terrified that something might happen to our new baby while she was caring for him, and, quite frankly, so was I. Dan and I decided that it was time for me to stay home with our young family. My older son was experiencing some social, bullying issues with classmates and needed his mom to help him as well. Fortunately, my husband's business had taken an extremely good turn, and he more than replaced my income, so we were able to become a single-income family.

We built a house in a new development. Most of the women were stay-at-home mothers, so it was easy to assimilate into a life with these wonderful people, making playdates, throwing pizza and ice cream parties, turning snow days into great memories, going on countless vacations together, and giving our kids wonderful childhood memories.

With all of this going on, it was also easy to stuff the dreams for myself down someplace deep inside of me. Let me be clear though. I would never have traded the gift, the opportunity to be home with my children, especially when they really needed me. However, that doesn't negate the fact that there was a woman, who came from a humble, limited beginning, who had an opportunity to make a mark on the world, especially in a place where I was so comfortable and rocked it! However, I stopped doing it and didn't see it through to fruition.

When the demands of motherhood settled down a bit, I decided to reinvent myself in 2004. My kids were still home, and I couldn't commit to 12-hour days in New York City, so I repurposed my work situation by becoming a consultant in the industry. This has worked out extremely well, except for the isolation. For quite some time, I've been working from home, building this business, yet feeling isolated because more or less I'm alone all day—not interacting, entertaining, and seeing clients as I'd done in years past. Mostly, I sat by my computer during a very long day, sending emails, and it can be boring. Although I've been successful with the current company I consult for, I don't feel the sense of connection, teamwork, and comradery that was once an integral part of my life.

Skip forward a couple of years, and the health issues started, so dreams were pushed farther away, and survival became the primary goal—survival, not for me but for those around me, who would be devastated if something happened to me. After Marianne's death and my first cancer diagnosis, I stopped worrying about my own mortality. I made peace with it, and I promised myself that, no matter how many people, physicians, or whoever tried to convince me, I would decline to start chemo—that poison. I would live the rest of the time allotted to me and then take whatever measures were available to die peacefully and humanely. This may not be the opinion of others, and I truly respect that, but it is mine, and I own and feel it completely.

I admire how simple and tranquil, and, of course, heart-breaking, it is to put a pet down at the veterinarian office, when their time comes. However, when it's time for our loved ones to leave us, they must go through days of unnecessary, insufferable, ongoing moments gasping for breath or thrashing in bed, oblivious to what was going on around them while their family members experienced unimaginable pain, leaving them completely depleted until the very last moment. Why?

After my double mastectomy, that was when I decided to become a life coach to help those who, like me, were struggling or stuck and needed to do the work, process it, and figure out how to make it through their journey.

However, I was a little depressed because I did not become who I set out to become, someone successful, admired, and written about; someone who was a mentor to others, an inspiration; someone with a Wikipedia page, as bizarre as that sounds. Looking back at this sentence (except about the Wiki page), I have become these things in my nuclear world in New Jersey; I can say this with assurance as I have, over time, been building out my life coach business. However, I wanted and, more than ever, want this NOW, particularly since I have been through two early stage cancer diagnoses, and I have been trying to figure out why I'm still here and how I can give back and teach others what I have learned about survival, internal strength, staring fear in the face, and converting it to power. Perhaps my goals are too lofty, but I want to share this not just locally but also with thousands of people around the country to help create meaningful change in those who seek out my voice and my story.

Something I'd like to share with you: *I've been doing a lot of research on mindfulness lately, and it's very interesting. I'm hoping if I try to stay in the present moment, living life by enjoying and taking in the beautiful things around me, not trying to control or predict the future, that there will be a shift in my path. I'm excited to share this with you as I continue on this journey.*

36

SO GOOD?

Two of my best friends started to go for colonics. They said that it was very healthy, very cleansing, and that it removes the toxins from your body. Once a month or so, they would go to some woman's house to have the procedure done.

One evening, while I was recuperating from the reconstructive surgery, they picked me up to take me out to dinner and began speaking about their experience, which occurred earlier that day. My initial thought was: you went together to have this colonic done? And the procedure occurs in someone's house, not an office or medical center? Yuck!!! Then I said to myself, "Stop it, Rosie, try to be open minded."

My friend Maribel said, "I had mine first, and it was SO GOOD."

Noreen chimed in with, "Me too. Mine was SO GOOD."

This conversation went on for a while, with each extolling the benefits and pleasure they received from having the colonics. That's when I lost my ability to hold my tongue. "SO

GOOD, SO GOOD? I'm sorry, but 'SO GOOD' is having an orgasm. 'SO GOOD' is a great meal, a good movie, seeing an interesting play, reading a fantastic book, or a recent vacation for that matter. 'SO GOOD' is not having an enema!"

"No, Rosa, you don't understand," Maribel said. "You feel so clean and empty and light after the colonic."

"Hmm, how much do you pay this woman to perform this magical procedure on you?" I inquired.

"Sixty dollars a session," Noreen replied.

After thinking for a few moments, I said, "I'll tell you what, the next time you feel the need to be cleansed, come to my house, and I will feed you sautéed broccoli rabe with garlic and oil and two glasses of wine. I promise you that, the next morning, not only will you be completely cleaned out, you can probably go for a colonoscopy that day if you want to. I won't even charge you anything! Plus, you won't have to have someone snake a tube up your ass!"

For some strange reason, they never brought up colonics to me ever again!

37

HOUSE CLEANING

I went over to my mom's place to visit with her. As I always do, I asked for the key to her room so I could check to make sure it was clean. I looked around and saw there were papers, magazines, and projects she had made during her various activities strewn throughout her apartment. I decided to take some time to get rid of some of the stuff that she wouldn't miss, since my fanatically neat mother in years past, was now incapable of doing this herself. I filled a large garbage bag with things she no longer needed.

When I went through her closet to pull out and hide shirts that she had been wearing over and over again because she no longer had the ability to remember what she last wore, I saw something shiny in the right-hand corner of the floor. I picked it up and smiled. It was a dime. Even when I'm sad, thinking about how different my mom is now and how much has changed in our lives, I'm reminded by the dimes when they magically appear that I'm on the path that I'm meant to be on.

I came home after my visit, checked my emails, and found there were two new inquiries about my life coaching services. I responded to both and secured the initial session for each. I had a gut feeling that I may be on my way to something that could potentially be bigger than I originally anticipated.

38

TATTOOS

*T*wo little circles. How can it be that two little circles can make me feel so complete?

When I started this mastectomy journey, I had so many different emotions and fears about having my breasts removed. I remember the last time my husband and I made love before the surgery; I realized that this would be the last time I would have erotic sensations from having him touch my nipples. I mourned that loss, as it was definitely a part of our foreplay, and I was angry that I had to give it up.

However, once my breasts and nipples were gone, there was something else that I was mourning. Many women say that one of the hardest parts of having a mastectomy is the first time you see yourself in the mirror and realize your breasts are gone. I must admit that this was very difficult for me, and I almost threw up when I saw a full-frontal view of myself. Over the months and during the saline fills, I watched my breasts slowly reappear, and then, when we swapped the expanders for the implants, I thought I would feel complete.

But something was missing. Two little circles, two little circles . . . my nipples. Every day, when I got out of the shower, my eyes focused on the incision lines from the major surgeries and the dings and dents from the biopsies and lumpectomies that occurred prior to the mastectomy. I focused on the imperfections that reminded me of all I had gone through. Of course, I felt blessed and thankful that I was alive, and I prayed every day, after having survived two cancer journeys, that these traumatic experiences were behind me and I could move on. Nonetheless, I did not see breasts when I looked in the mirror, but instead I saw the scars from my journey.

My husband and I had many discussions on whether I should have nipple reconstruction, where a surgeon would take skin from other parts of my body, called donor sites, to reconstruct my nipples, or whether I would get 3-D tattoos. I decided to go with the tattoos for many reasons, with the most prevalent one being that I did not want to have any more surgeries. After four biopsies, three lumpectomies, countless mammograms, ultrasounds and MRIs, a double mastectomy, and then reconstructive surgery, I did not want to have to recover from another procedure. 3-D nipple tattooing took one hour, from start to finish.

On May 3rd, we arrived at a famous 3-D tattoo parlor just prior to our 1 p.m. appointment. It was in Maryland, which was a 3.5-hour drive for us. I told my husband he had to be my wingman, making sure that each nipple went on each breast in the same spot. The last thing I needed was to have my nipples looking like Igor's eyes from *Young Frankenstein*, with one looking one way and the other looking another.

After filling out some routine paperwork, we were told that the tattoo artist, Vinnie, was ready for us, and we were brought into a small room and waited for him to arrive. Besides his signature hat that he seemed to always wear, the one thing that stood out about him was his piercing blue eyes. Over the years, Vinnie has worked with thousands of women to create and complete nipples for breasts that were interrupted by cancer, and I could not help but think that those blue eyes have guided him in each of his works of art.

We quickly got to work. He asked me to stand in front of him, and he began to draw circles in the places he thought my nipples might look best. Being the super prepared, obsessive person, I am, I whipped out photos of my original nipples for comparison's sake to show him what I was aiming for. After a couple of tweaks, we all agreed as to where they would look best, and he started the procedure.

Many people asked me if it hurt during the tattooing, and, to my surprise, it was mildly uncomfortable but completely overshadowed by the fun, lighthearted conversation that my husband, Vinnie, and I had during our hour-long visit. He shared that he had four children, and we swapped stories about how much college cost and how hard we collectively worked as parents to get our kids through it without them incurring enormous debt when they graduated. We joked and talked about many things, which made the hour pass quickly. When all was done with the first nipple, he swiveled my chair around so I could take a look in a full-length mirror, and, whoa, I could not believe what I saw. I saw my breasts take on a new incredible look, one which I had not seen since before this journey began. I did not see the scars, the dings, the dents, or the imperfections. Instead, I saw a real-looking breast, and it made me feel complete and happy. With our thumbs-up, Vinnie went on to create a mirror image on my other breast.

I do not think I'm a superficial person, and I completely recognize that these new nipples were not going to be publicly displayed. I was a 53-year-old married woman and mother. I was not going to show them to the world—in a wet tee-shirt contest or whatever—and the only people who will likely see them will be me, my husband, and my physician. Furthermore, I realized that they do not serve a useful function in my life. I will not be nursing and nurturing a baby. Essentially, they were there for me and only for me.

Once he was finished, we thanked Vinnie for his work, and off he went to help the next woman who had come to him to find closure and completion. I remember during the car ride home taking a peek at my nipples every 15 minutes or so and laughing, not in a HA HA way, but more in a "Woo hoo, this is great!" kind of way.

Chapter Takeaway: In a screwed-up situation when you have to do something so extreme such as removing your breasts, albeit for the most important reason to potentially save your life, there is something nice to be said about having someone who can bring some confidence and happiness to you with his incredible talent and eyes of perfection. Tomorrow, I will wake up and no longer feel damaged; I will feel a little more complete. A step toward getting better!

I find this quote to be very soothing:

"You aren't what's happened to you, you are how you've overcome it." – Beau Taplin

39

VENTING A BIT

*I*f people took the time to really know me, they would know what is important to me and what is not. I'm not a materialistic person. I don't feel important and have an increased self-worth when I wear a piece of clothing with someone's famous name on it. I feel good when I wear something that looks good on me, and that can come from Costco, Kohl's, or a boutique shop.

What IS important to me, and what I wish my loved ones would **HEAR HEAR HEAR** is that life experiences are important to me. A great meal, a fun show, a rockin' concert, a wine tasting, a cooking class, a comedy club, a great play, a special day, hopefully many, with my family—Dan, Greg, Jordan, Greg's girlfriend Allie, and me—where we sit and joke and poke fun at each other and reminisce about the life we built together.

This, as well as when I feel appreciated by my family for

what I do for them and how much I think of them first before myself, makes me happy.

Last night, we went out to dinner with the kids, including Marianne's son, and my husband inadvertently knocked a glass over, and it shattered. We all clapped and hugged because we knew that Marianne was with us.

Today, Dan and I went for a walk on the boardwalk at the Jersey Shore. He randomly parked in a spot, and, when we got out of the car, we looked at the spot number so that we could pay at the parking meter, and it was #311, March 11th, Marianne's birthday—another "wink" from her telling me that she has been with me this entire journey. I took a picture of it and sent it to Geri, another very close friend of Marianne's and mine. She cried upon receiving it because she has always called Marianne a strong and present angel and knew she was beside me.

40

CHECKMATE!

Following my 3-D nipple tattoos, everyone wanted to see my tits, including my family practitioner. At an appointment following my procedure, the first thing she asked was how everything went. She asked if they looked real, and she kept looking down at my breasts. She wouldn't flat out say she wanted to see them, but I could tell from her body language that she was dying to see how they turned out. After deliberating in my head for a couple of minutes, I decided to give her a hall pass, as I figured that she could potentially help another patient debating about whether to have tattoos versus some other option. So, I flashed her. Thus far, she and Dan are the only two people who have seen them. All three of us were amazed by Vinnie's work.

For the rest of my social circle, many of them have nonchalantly said that they would like to see the results of the 3-D nipple tattooing, but it was said in such a casual way, as if they would like to see my newly remodeled bathroom. But, NO! This is not how this was going to go down. I set the ground rules. I told each that inquired, "If you want to see my breasts, you will need to show me yours first. If I'm going to be in a vulnerable situation, you need to be in it too." In other words, if you want to see my nipples and reconstructed breasts, which come along with my scars, dings, and dents from all I've been through, you must show me your tits first. Alas, these super interested friends needed to think a moment to decide whether they wanted me to see their 50-something-year-old breasts, some of which were sagging from aging, gravity, and nursing. Thus far, none of the above have asked me again.

When I first decided to create the rules for what someone needed to share with me before I revealed what I had going on, I told Dan that, to show my breasts with all of the busy work that had occurred, I needed to up the stakes and tell them they needed to show me a full frontal view of their vagina. But then I thought long and hard about this and said to myself, "Do you really want to see someone's 50-something-year-old vagina that's been ravaged by childbirth and worn out from years of overuse? Yuck!" I decided to keep it to "You show me your tits first, and then I'll show you mine!"

41

COMPLETELY DEVASTATING!

One thing I know for sure as a result of this journey is that I can never, ever say to my husband (and I'm having major trepidation just writing it), "You know, Dan, I'm feeling peaceful. I'm starting to feel alive," because as soon as I say it, BOOM, I get knocked to the ground again.

During Labor Day weekend of 2016, I was feeling like I was turning a corner and things were settling down a bit. Something that always lifts me up and makes me feel better is walking on the boardwalk near the Jersey Shore. I cannot tell you how many miles I've logged in my sneakers, walking and walking with my husband during my cancer diagnosis, through my mother's decline and eventual difficult entry into an assisted living facility, and during my mastectomy and reconstructive surgery recoveries.

So, on the Monday of the Labor Day weekend, September 5th, 2016, Dan suggested we take a walk in Long Branch to check out the waves brought on by the tail end of Hurricane

Hermine. When we arrived, I vividly remember being frightened for the crazy teenagers who stood out on the jetties as the waves crashed against them. I was afraid they would be instantly swept away into the ocean.

From a completely different perspective, I marveled at how powerful the ocean was and how thankful I was that we live so close by and can enjoy its beauty. We stood together for a long time, holding hands, watching the ocean and the moonlight casting a shimmering glow on its surface.

We came home at around 10:00 p.m., and I settled in by pouring myself a glass of wine and turning on the TV. At 10:34 p.m., the phone rang, and the caller ID showed it was my brother Carl. This was unusual because Carl is an early riser and usually goes to bed around 9:30 p.m. I immediately thought that something happened to my mom and perhaps her nursing staff had called him, but that would be odd because he lives in South Carolina, and I live 10 minutes away from her. I answered the phone and said, "Hi, Carl." But it wasn't Carl on the line. The person on the cell phone said, "Hi, this is Carl's father-in-law. I'm so sorry to have to call you with this news, but there has been a terrible accident. Carl was rehearsing for the opening of the new play he's in, and he fell off the stage and hit his head. They think he may have broken his neck, and they say there's only a 10 percent chance he'll survive."

Tears, panic, fear, and sobbing sounds that I didn't even know I was capable of making—that was all I remember. How could this have happened? Carl moved to South Carolina a couple of years back with his wife after retiring early from a lucrative career. He began auditioning for parts in local theatre with a passion. Just a few weeks before the accident, he proudly shared on Facebook that he had been cast in the play *"You Can't Take It with You"* at his community playhouse.

How did this happen? Carl's father-in-law went on to explain that my 58-year-old, healthy, happy, full-of-life brother was assisting another castmate in taking a table off of the stage when he accidentally walked backwards off the three foot stage and hit the back of his head on the concrete floor. He was conscious and verbal when the ambulance arrived, but the prognosis was bleak when he arrived at the hospital. One step backwards off a stage, immediate life-changing event in a split second. Oh my God, oh my God. How could this happen? I handed the phone to Dan because I couldn't breathe. I tried to stand up but felt dizzy.

Carl's father-in-law and Dan spoke for a little longer, but I really was not sure what they said. Then his father-in-law asked to speak to me again and what he asked me to do made me have to pull myself together. He asked me to call my niece, my brother's daughter, to inform her what happened. He said that Carl's wife, my niece's stepmom, was too overcome with grief to do so. Once again, I needed to go into survival, composure mode, pull myself together, and make that call. That was probably one of the worst calls I've had to make in my life.

Early the next morning, Carl's father-in-law called to say that things were worse than they thought. An MRI had been performed on Carl in the middle of the night, and the doctors determined there was no brain activity. He was brain dead. My super smart brother who worked his way through night school to earn his bachelor's and master's degree in software engineering was no longer with us. His father-in-law suggested we gather our stuff together and book the next flight to South Carolina to say our goodbyes. The hospital would keep him on life support until the entire family arrived, which included my sister, brother-in-law, and Carl's daughter and her new husband.

What followed was more tears, an inability to breathe, and dizzy spells—but somehow I managed to put some clothes in a bag, and Dan booked a flight and hotel for us. I called my children, reluctantly shared this terrible news, and told them to prepare to come back to New Jersey as we planned to hold a Mass and gathering at our house after we returned from South Carolina. That was another heart-wrenching call to make, having to break this news to my sons.

My sister and I spoke before we boarded the flight, and, after a bit of discussion, we agreed that we would not tell our mother about this tragic loss. She'd already buried one son, and, at her advanced stage of dementia, nothing positive would come from us telling her that she lost another child.

I don't really remember much about the trip to South Carolina. I'm not a great flyer, and I usually worry about turbulence or the plane crashing, but this time none of this entered my mind. Plus, when we took off, I looked at the time, and it was 3:11 p.m., another indication that my friend Marianne was with us. I do remember that I cried when we took off and cried as we landed. I was crying about something so unfathomable, so painful, and raw. I was thinking about life, my brother's life, and how, in one split second, everything changed so permanently and dramatically. This tragic loss is still incomprehensible to me. It has left me with a deep, aching hole in my heart. I couldn't believe that this happened, and that it occurred just seven months after my double mastectomy—what I thought at the time was the most life-altering event in my life. I believe I will grieve the loss of Carl for the remainder of my life, as I have grieved for Tommy, my first sibling to pass in 1993, at the age of 38.

We landed, headed to the hotel, and tried to get some sleep. The next day, Dan and I would go to the hospital with the rest of the family to say goodbye to Carl, who was legally declared dead the day before, but has been kept breathing so his family could feel he was still with us.

Just two days before, I worried about the teenagers on the jetty being swept away, not knowing that my brother Carl would be the one to be taken from us suddenly that evening.

42

A GATHERING

My sister-in-law decided to throw a celebration of Carl's life while we, his family, were there and after we said our goodbyes, so that all his friends, family, and coworkers who lived nearby could come to pay their respects. She picked a charming wine bar, which was quite lovely, and they put out some food, which looked nice, although I had no appetite at all, so I could only assume it was good.

Shortly after arriving, I was overwhelmed by the amount of people who had come to mourn, pay their respects, and, in a more positive frame of mind, share stories about how Carl had touched their lives.

Backing up a little bit, I was a little upset when my brother decided to leave Connecticut and his family and relocate to South Carolina. I especially became more resentful as my mother declined, and it became apparent that he would be with her two, possibly four, days a year vs. having an active, day-to-day role in her health issues.

When I was among his people, I saw a different side of his life that I hadn't realized existed. Truthfully, I was a total mess and told Dan to find me a table because I was incapable of standing on my own due to these unexplainable waves of dizziness. A glass of wine later, however, and I was ready to interact with his friends.

The beautiful thing is that I didn't need to stand up and mingle. Thank goodness, because I didn't have the strength to do so. Since I learned about his tragic accident, the unexpected dizzy spells became terrible and uncontrollable. Fortunately, the people in his social circle sought us out and sat with us to share what Carl meant to them. I learned that one woman really wanted to perform in local theatre but had terrible stage fright, and my brother gave her a chance, coached her through her worries, and helped her get to the point of being part of her first performance, under his direction. I learned that work colleagues at the Golf Shop relied on him for guidance and support. I learned from the director of shows that he performed in that he felt he was an integral part of the team and a major factor in the success of the shows they produced, feedback that would make him so proud.

I also learned more about his passion for being an organ donor from his pastor and that this was so important to him as he hoped to help or save others when he died. I vividly remember Carl saying, on the rare occasions that we discussed our wishes after we died, "I don't give a rat's ass what's done with my body after I'm gone, as long as my organs go to people who might benefit from them!"

43

CARL'S MEMORIAL SERVICE

My eyes opened this morning, and I already knew that the only way to make it through today was with Xanax. Today was Carl's memorial service at St. B's Roman Catholic church, back home in New Jersey. Because of Facebook, numerous phone calls, and emails, we were going to have a very big turnout at the church. There would be so many people who, over the years, had been friends with Carl, work colleagues, family members, and people whose lives, in one way or another, he had touched.

Prior to the memorial service, my friend Val spent over an hour on the phone with my niece Ciana and I, gathering info that we would want to share about Carl during the service. Since Ciana was his only daughter, I was a passive participant, as I wanted her to impart the important elements of his life, information she wanted those who attended to learn about him. There were two things that most people did not know, that she wanted to include in the service: The first was that Carl was very passionate about being an organ donor, and, remarkably, when he died, he helped or saved over 100 people because he was so physically fit! The other intriguing thing was that he and his long-time friend Ed had challenged each other years ago to see who could be the first to visit each of the 50 states in our country. I remember many years earlier, when our kids were little, and we went to Park City, Utah, to ski as a family, Carl woke up at 3:00 a.m. to drive to Wyoming so he could check that off of his bucket list and be back in time to hit the slopes with his daughter and my sons. The younger people at the memorial service thought this was a really cool bucket list agenda, and some vowed to keep it going in honor of Carl.

As I got ready for the service and made my way downstairs, I told my older son Greg I couldn't breathe, that I was having a hard time standing up due to these unexplained dizzy spells, and that I wasn't sure how I was going to walk into the church, seeing all of these faces, present and past, especially past. These are one of the times when you see the love come through from your kids, where they stop what they're doing, not think about themselves, but recognize that their mom, their rock, needs them to be the strong one. Greg sat with me while I cried and shook. He told me once again that I was the strongest person he knew, then he hugged me and somehow (with the Xanax) he, Dan, Jordan, and Greg's girlfriend Allie helped me get into the car and make it to the service.

There were no less than 150 people in the church that day, there for my brother Carl—high school friends, work colleagues, family, my friends—all heartbroken that a life could be stolen, so tragically and senselessly, at 58 years old. To say I was a mess would be an understatement. With all the adversity I've encountered in my life, I think I have only really fallen apart, completely unraveled, during two people's deaths, and that was with Marianne in 2004 and Carl in 2016—the first because she was so young, full of life, and was leaving behind two small children, the other because Carl's death was such a senseless and tragic accident. I have lost many significant people in my life, but I have been better prepared for their deaths because I knew they were coming.

So much crying and grief occurred before we entered the Chapel—until the priest announced we needed to get started. I must say it was a lovely service and tribute to my brother's life. Since I was in a completely altered state, it was only afterwards that my close friends told me that so many people were emotionally affected by the service, sitting quietly crying as the priest and others spoke about Carl. I have my friend Val, her husband Tom, and Ciana, my beautiful niece, to thank for pulling this off—and for St. B's for accepting and welcoming us on such short notice, particularly since we were not parishioners.

44

REPAST

After the Mass, we headed back to our house for the repast. My wonderful neighbors and family put together the food. Since we spent a lot of time at the church saying goodbye and thank you to those who weren't coming back, we were essentially the last people to arrive at the gathering. As is the case with my go-to people, they had it all under control—the food was unwrapped, people were happily eating, and all was going well. Ciana mentioned that she wanted to say some special words about her dad, Popi, as she called him, and I told her that the timing, based on many years of experience in hosting gatherings, would be to do so directly, after people ate and before dessert. She was so articulate, poised, and poignant and really gave those in the room, which consisted of about 100 people, a sense of who her father was and what he meant to her. I was completely awestruck and proud of her!

I decided to open the room, the floor, to anyone who wanted

to share a story, event, or memory of Carl, but I wasn't sure if this was going to create a meaningful exchange or become a dead duck, with no one wanting to contribute. Luckily, many people stood up and shared. The real stand out ones were when Carl's high school friends told stories, which brought me back to a time that was simpler, zany, didn't make much sense, but now makes you laugh out loud. Perhaps the most profound share came from a man, whom no one knew, but who turned out to be a work colleague of Carl's, at the company he worked for in NYC for over 25 years. This guy shared that my brother was a manager and was hiring for a specific role many, many years ago that required a college degree, something that this gentleman did not have. However, my brother saw something in him and decided to make the hire. The most interesting information that this man shared was that my brother taught him something related to software engineering approximately 20 years ago—which is above my knowledge and pay grade—that he still uses to teach his new hires today. In fact, he continued to share that he had used this info the week before Carl's passing to teach one of his new hires. I was honored that this man, my brother's colleague, traveled from his home in Connecticut to New Jersey to attend the Mass. Additionally, he took time from his day and decided to come back to our house to share this significant story with us, demonstrating another beautiful, unsolicited act of kindness by him and also by my brother for taking a leap of faith with this man many years ago.

I find this quote to be very soothing:

"Kindness can be the greatest gift that you can give a person. Especially when they're not expecting it." – RAKtivist

45

CARL AND MY MOTHER

When we learned about the tragic accident, my sister and I had a conversation about what we would do with our mother. After a lengthy discussion, we agreed that, at this stage in her dementia, we were not going to tell her that Carl had died. She has no conception of time, forgets what happened the day before or even an hour before, and her knowing this terrible news might destroy her. We already watched her bury one child when our brother Tommy died in 1993 at 38 years old—and that was just awful. No mother should ever have to bury a child, and we were determined to shelter her from having to bury another. The only good thing about her having dementia is that we could get away with this. When she innocently asked me, "I haven't heard from Carl lately?" I would just respond, "You told me you spoke to him a couple of days ago." I have learned to become a very convincing liar, something I'm not proud of, but I had to figure out how to do it. She then would look deep into my eyes—I make sure to not waver or falter—and then she says, "Oh, I forgot." And the conversation ends there.

My heart sinks when I lie, but I know it's for the best, and, at this stage of her dementia, we can pull it off. It sucks to be so deceptive but taking care of someone you love and protecting them from a painful, unfathomable truth weighs higher on the scale than the alternative option.

After these visits with her, the lying always weighed heavy on me for some reason. Whenever this happened, I started to think about this, as well as all that has happened thus far this year, and my head would feel like it was going to explode.

I was having a hard time closing my eyes at night and began drinking wine to help me get to sleep. After a couple of days of pondering all of this, I decided that I couldn't do it alone and needed some help and guidance. The next day, I called and made an appointment to see a therapist.

46

A PACKAGE ARRIVED

*A*bout two weeks after Carl passed away, I was getting back to my work routine and feeling thankful that things were pretty busy, as it was a welcome distraction from my grief. Dan popped into my office on Monday and handed me a card from the post office and said, "We missed a delivery. I think it's the Wee Wee Pads for the dogs. Will you have time today to pick them up?"

I answered, "I'm super busy and under deadline for a project, but I'll try to get to it."

For the next two days, Dan nudged me and inquired as to whether I could pick up the package. Finally, on Wednesday, I snapped at him, "For God's sake, it's a package of Wee Wee Pads. If it's so important, make your way over to the post office and get it yourself!"

As luck would have it, Wednesday was a beautiful day in late September, and my two afternoon conference calls had been rescheduled for the next day, so I found myself with a free afternoon. I picked up the phone and called my friend and said, "Hi, Annie, what are you up to today?"

She replied, "Not much, just running errands. What's up?"

I said, "Are you free to come shopping with me? I want to see if I can buy some new shirts from White House Black Market."

"Sure, what time are you thinking of heading to the mall?"

I told her, "I have to stop at the post office to pick up a package, but I can meet you around 2:30 p.m., if that works for you." We agreed to the time and hung up.

At around 2:00 p.m., I headed out with the slip of paper from the post office and called my cousin Lisa on the way to catch up. When I arrived at my destination, I told her I needed to hang up as I was next in line. I handed the slip to the postal worker; she walked to the storage area and came back placing a small box on the counter in front of me. I said to her, "There must be some mistake. The package I'm picking up is much larger than this."

Since there was a line of people behind me, and this must not have been the first time she has done this, she turned the box slightly, but in such a way that only I could read what was written on the front of it. I glanced down and all the blood drained from my face. I stammered and stuttered, "What? What? That's how they send this?" She didn't even respond. She just nodded her head yes.

What appeared on the front of the box in bold letters were the words: CREMATION REMAINS. The box was addressed to me, and it was sent from the funeral home that my brother was sent to after his organs were harvested for donation purposes and he was taken off life support and cremated.

Shock! I couldn't believe there was no notification—no

email, phone call, certified letter, or something that said, "Your loved one's cremation remains are being shipped to you and should arrive on or around the last week of September."

Shaking, I left the post office carrying what remained of my brother Carl and put him on the passenger seat of the car. I was having a hard time breathing and called Dan to tell him what had just happened. I said, "I just came from the post office to get the package you wanted me to get. It wasn't Wee Wee Pads. It was my brother Carl's remains!!!"

Dan replied, "What! That's how they send them! And with no advance notice?"

I responded, "Apparently so." I started to cry. "If I knew that this was what was waiting at the post office, I would have never waited two days to get the package, and I would have sent you to get it. I can't breathe!"

Dan told me to pull over as I was driving. We talked for a bit more, and, when I was calm enough to drive again, I hung up the phone and continued home. Again, shaking, I carried my brother into the house. I called Annie, my shopping buddy, before I reached my house to let her know what had just happened and that I wouldn't be able to make it to the mall. When I arrived home, she was at my driveway waiting to console me as she knew how distraught I was. Another blessing!

A little while later, I called Lisa back and told her what had occurred. I said, "Can you believe they sent my brother's remains via the US Postal Service? For God's sake, if I ordered a toaster, it would have been shipped via FedEx or UPS!"

Lisa replied, "What the fuck? I don't believe this!" Lisa is a research expert, and I knew that she would immediately get the 411 on why they had shipped Carl in such a manner. Sure enough, within 10 minutes of my sharing this story with her, she texted me two links showing that FedEx and UPS do not accept or ship cremation remains, and the only legal way to ship them is via the US Postal Service. Contrary to what we originally thought, we had not missed a package. The post office cannot deliver human remains directly to a residence. It has to be sent from the funeral home to the post office, and a card is sent to the intended recipient, letting them know that there is a package that needs to be picked up. Unfortunately, and inadvertently, I let my brother sit in the post office for two days because I thought I was picking up Wee Wee Pads for the dogs.

From late September, the year he passed, until June of the next year, Carl remained in the house with us. One day, when I was feeling very blue, I asked his daughter, my niece, if she wanted the remains to reside in her house. At around this time, she had learned that she was pregnant with her first child and now had a strong feeling of wanting her father to be close by. We agreed to ship him, again via the US Postal Service, but this time the recipient, my niece and her husband, were aware that Carl was on his way.

47

THERAPY

I set an appointment for this Thursday at 1:30 p.m. with my new psychologist, Dr. Cheryl Weinstein—another Jewish therapist. Come to think of it, through the years, I have only seen Jewish therapists.

I said to Dan, "Aren't there any Italian psychologists out there?" Then I thought for a moment and answered my own question, "There aren't any Italian therapists for one big reason."

"And what's that?" Dan inquired.

"Because an Italian psychologist would only see someone for two sessions before he or she said to the patient, 'How about I take a baseball bat to your skull and bash your brains in! Then you won't be so caught up with your silly fucking problems!!!'"

My husband just shook his head, sighed, and walked away from me. This was one of the by-products of the year I'd had: I'd totally lost my filter, and my mind went to the most twisted places—funny, but twisted.

48

REFLECTION

*L*ast night, Jordan was sharing with me the details surrounding the tragedy of a young man who died at his college at one of the frat houses. This boy was pledging one of the fraternities—pledging is a variety of things that someone trying to enter the frat has to do to gain entry. From the news articles written about the incident, the boy was really drunk as a result of some hazing ritual, and the members of that fraternity allegedly did not seek out proper care for him when he fell down the stairs. In reading further, it came out that he was so drunk that he could not even stand up, yet the other frat members did not take him to the hospital to seek proper medical attention. The same article indicated that, due to the fall, he ruptured his spleen and sustained head injuries. I started to think about this kid's parents, who were likely home going about their normal routine for that evening, not knowing what was happening to their son and how they would have given anything to have been able to step in to help if they could have had the opportunity.

Grief strikes at the most unexpected times. After Jordan shared this story, I started to think about my brother and what occurred the night of his tragic accident. When we were in South Carolina for the memorial gathering his wife put together after his passing, one of my brother's castmates from the play came to sit with us for a while. This gentleman shared that, when Carl fell off the stage and hit his head, he was in the Green Room, helping with lighting and feeding the cast their lines. He heard one of the actor's yell, "call 911" and thought to himself that this was odd, as it was not a line in the script. He and the rest of the crew rushed to the stage to find Carl sitting in one of the seats set up for the audience. Carl asked this gentleman and a few others to help him get to the bathroom, as he was unable to walk unassisted. When he got there, he vomited, and this guy, who was also a paramedic, recognized that this was not a good sign for someone with a head injury. My brother was so polite, always one to assist but not likely to seek out help; I can only imagine how he gently requested their help.

He further shared that a few of the men waited with Carl, who was still conscious and verbal at this time, until the ambulance arrived. I have been told that, when Carl got to the hospital, he lost his ability to speak and respond to verbal commands from the emergency room team, was still able to move his extremities on cue, but, a short time later, he became brain dead. Although I'm not completely certain of the exact timeline, I know the outcome.

An overwhelming feeling of sadness came over me. My

brother Carl was one of the most polite, helpful, giving people I have ever known. It makes perfect sense that, when asked to assist with moving the table off the stage, he would have been the first to volunteer to do so. While I try not to dwell on how this tragedy occurred because I know it was an accident, I still find my mind drifting to the question, "How is it that no one saw him walking backwards toward the edge of the stage, particularly the person facing forward holding the other side of the table?"

I thought of my brother, so independent and the first to help, politely asking for assistance to make it to the bathroom after the accident, and it made me cry. As Paul McCartney wrote, "Let It Be," but many times when I found myself in a dark, grief-stricken place, playing out the senselessness of this tragic accident, I had a hard time doing so.

My new therapist said these are the times when I must take out my journal and write about the feelings I have, write about how angry and bitter I am, write and write until my hand feels like it's going to fall off—as ugly as the thoughts might be. I do this, but my thoughts seem to circle back to one thing: How did the person walking forward with the table not notice that he or she was leading my brother to the edge of the stage and not notice that he was about to fall off?

When I returned from South Carolina, many people asked me if I tried to seek that person out to garner a better understanding of how the unfathomable could have happened. I did not, and there are two reasons why: By knowing the answer, I could not change the outcome and bring my brother back, and, in meeting me or any other of our family members, if broached with this question, we could not make this person feel any worse than he or she already felt. What would be the purpose of inflicting more pain than already existed for this individual?

I knew that I really needed this week's therapy session on Thursday.

49

MARIANNE AGAIN

Last night, I was watching TV, and a promo came on for a new TV show. The lyrics from the group Boston's song "More Than a Feeling" were playing in the background, and I heard them sing, "I see my Marianne walking away." Back in 2003, while she was ill, and in 2004, when she passed, I distinctly remember these lyrics because metaphorically this song always reminds me of my friend "walking away" or leaving us when she died. Then the announcer said that the show was going to premiere in the spring on March 11th, Marianne's birthday, and I just laughed. She knew I needed her nearby.

50

HOMEWORK

Somewhere during this journey, I started to believe I hated myself. I mentioned this to my therapist on a couple of occasions, and, one day, she called me out on it. "It's unsettling to me that you keep mentioning this. Why do you feel you hate yourself?"

Because I wasn't able to come up with something on the spot, she asked me to do a homework assignment. She said, "I want you to take a piece of paper and draw a line down the center so that there are two columns, with the first being what you like about yourself, and the second being what you dislike. Then come back next week, and we will discuss this list."

Being the good Catholic school student I was, I took a deep dive into this list, trying to be as honest as I could about my feelings. Here's what I came up with:

What I like about myself:

I'm funny (really Rosie, that's the first thing to come to your mind!)

Loving, compassionate

Good—maybe a great mother

Good wife, loyal; we have stayed together through all our challenges for 35 years

Very good friend

I'm the rock that keeps the family together and do it with ease, hosting most, if not all, family gatherings.

Loved by many people

Have kept people in my life since childhood

Good daughter

I mostly don't put up with people's bullshit, and when people try to disrespect me, they get "Rosie'd"*

Smart

Good writer. I write so that the reader can feel what I'm describing

Love my husband/committed relationship

He adores me and we have good—sometimes great sex

Good cook

Adventurous and loves to find new things to do, places to go and see, and I love sharing this with others

<u>What I hate about myself:</u>

Many struggles, such as gluten allergy, bleeding disorder, cancer twice, sleep issues

Way too many surgeries, and I tested positive for four cancer genes

Things don't usually go smoothly for me; I have to fight so hard that I often feel cursed

My brother Tommy and Carl's deaths as well as other heartbreaking losses such as my sister-in-law Kathy, and Marianne's passing

Hard to face my anxiety and fears

Lonely and bored sometimes, and trying to figure out who I am and why I'm still here if not to do something positive after the adversity I've faced

Haven't reached the potential of who I want to be

Secluded, isolated job

Fear of driving on the parkway after the mastectomy

I don't know who I am

After I read both lists to my therapist, she said to me, "When you read the things you like about yourself, are they empty words on a page or do you really believe them to be true?"

I had to admit that I did believe they were true. Then she asked me a pivotal question.

"So, if you believe in the things that you like about yourself, how can you say that you hate yourself? You may hate what happened to you, and there's no denying that you've experienced enormously challenging events, but to say you hate yourself? I don't think that this is what you're really feeling." This was eye opening for me, and another move toward turning the corner.

Thereafter, I started paying more attention to the positive sides of the list. How could I expand upon them and focus less on the negative parts? As she shared, "These are thing that happened to you, that you can't change; somehow, you had the strength to make it through them, but now they're in your past."

*By definition, getting "Rosie'd" is being told off in a way in which I methodically pull apart the bullshit someone is serving up to me piece by piece, prove them wrong, and make the person who has the audacity to try to manipulate me walk away from the conversation with their head spinning.

51

MORE DIMES

Today I found two dimes, one on the floor in my garage, and one in the parking lot near my favorite clothing store. This inspired me to continue to move forward, building my life coaching and motivational speaking business. I wrote in my journal what I read earlier about finding dimes: *Finding dimes is guidance or validation from your guardian angels that you're on the right path.* I have my website set up. I just hired a person to build out my social media platforms, and I'm making connections for speaking engagements. All I can say is, "Bring it on!"

I find this quote to be very soothing:

> *"Faith is taking the first step, even if you don't see the entire staircase." – Martin Luther King, Jr.*

52

NOTHING LIKE A NEW BABY

The baby was coming. The baby was coming very soon. Our Ciana, Carl's daughter, was having a baby, and we would all soon have a little girl to spoil and love in our lives. However, she would not really know us well because she would live far away in Colorado, but we planned to go visit as often as possible because my niece and her new young family live there, and they were not planning to come back here to live. We made a commitment to go to Colorado as frequently as we could to visit and FaceTime often so that the baby would know Uncle Dan and Aunt Rosie, especially because I was her grandfather's sister, and I planned to do my part to keep Carl alive in her life, as I was certain Ciana and her husband Blaine would do as well.

And speaking of which, Carl would have been so happy to be having a grandchild, a beautiful baby girl, another one to call "the kid," his nickname for Ciana. I wholeheartedly believe that, with his flexible semi-retirement schedule, he would have been visiting frequently, showering the baby with love and coddling her.

The baby was coming, and this was such a huge blessing; this innocent little girl would come into our beautiful niece and nephew's life and forever change their world. As parents, they would have to navigate a different path, one that involves sacrifices, spur of the moment changes, sleeplessness, and euphoria over simple things like when the baby poops after a few days of not doing so and is experiencing discomfort. As parents, Ciana and Blaine would feel their child's pain and angst more than they do. But the joy, the love, and unconditional feeling of "wow, how did I live without her in my life," this was your future. I could not wait for Ciana, the first baby born on my side of the family when I was in my early 20s, to receive this gift.

This beautiful baby entered our lives on December 11th, 2017. I cried when I saw the first photos of her being held by her elated parents. I reminisced about the two happiest days of our lives, when Greg and Jordan were born, changing our lives forever. Ciana and Blaine have chosen to name her Maea, and we cannot wait to meet this special little person who has brought our family such an amazing, joyful gift, something we have not experienced in quite some time.

Chapter Takeaway: *The funny thing about love is that it can rush over you immediately, and you can feel a profound deep connection when something like this happens, especially the miracle of having a new baby enter your life. This is powerful.*

I find this quote to be very soothing:

"A new baby is the beginning of all things—wonder, hope, a dream of possibilities" – Eda J. Le Shan

53

PROCESSING GRIEF

This topic has probably been debated for quite some time. On the one hand, when someone you love passes away, is it harder to know that they're sick and watch the progression of their illness until the time comes for them to leave you? Does that give you time to prepare for the fact that they will no longer be in your life?

Or, on the other hand, can a sudden unexpected death be just as devastating, perhaps more? When someone you love dies unexpectedly, especially if it's a freak accident, how do you process, grieve it, and try to make peace with it? This was a question I asked myself over and over following Carl's tragic accident.

When I received the phone call regarding my brother Carl's tragic accident on September 5th, 2016, my world changed forever. I was brought to my knees and crushed in a way I never knew was possible. I think of these school and movie theatre shootings, cars and trucks running people over, or an insane person shooting innocent people from his hotel room as they simply sat on a lawn watching a concert. And then I think of the countless European tragedies, yet again resulting in people, special people who were so important and loved by their families, dying suddenly in an unfathomable way. How do we process this loss?

I've been on both sides of the spectrum, watching people diagnosed with a terminal illness and witnessing their decline and eventual passing, and I also have experienced an unexpected death of a close family member, especially when it makes no sense, and it occurs in a split second. Unfortunately, we cannot rewind the clock, change the circumstances, and save any of them. Loss is tragic and heartbreaking, and it takes time to move toward healing.

54

REMINISCING

My therapist suggested I use my journal not only as a vehicle to release sad thoughts but also to record happy ones as well.

Earlier today, I began thinking about a simple, less complex time, when I was in my teens, and Carl was in his early 20s. We both had some problems that required care from a dermatologist. I started to have some wicked acne, and, he, unfortunately, started to lose his hair. Someone recommended we see Dr. Y, and we both started weekly treatment for our respective problems. My protocols were acid peels, which left my face looking like a burn victim, not exactly what you want or how you want your face to look like in your junior year of high school.

Carl's treatment for his hair loss was that Dr. Y would give him an injection in his butt cheeks each week, and this was supposed to stimulate hair growth on his head. After a couple of months, we compared notes. Thankfully, my acne had started to subside. Unfortunately, Carl's situation hadn't worked out as expected. He said, "I don't have one new hair on my head, but I have a ponytail growing out of my ass from the injections."

We both fell to the floor laughing.

55

FACETIME CHAT

I visited my mom today and showed her pictures of the baby, Carl's granddaughter, my mom's great-granddaughter. I was so angry that Carl was not here to enjoy his beautiful granddaughter. I had to LIE to my mother about Carl, the baby, and whether Carl was happy to be a grandfather.

I would always check my mom's room when I visit to make sure it was clean, and the first thing I'd see is Ciana's wedding photo, where Carl proudly walked her down the aisle. Who knew that he had less than 11 months to live at that point? Death caused by a senseless accident, not by a disease or a premeditated circumstance. This is not to say that these are less significant or devastating, and I do cry when I watch what's going on in our world today or remember loved ones who have died from cancer. But, in my world, my personal world, my brother walked backwards off a fucking three-foot stage, hit his head on a cement floor, and was rendered brain dead shortly thereafter.

I go insane sometimes when I think about how this happened. I have to keep this lie going, look straight into my mother's innocent blue eyes, and spin a web of deceit—all for the right reasons. But it doesn't make it suck any less.

Carl's daughter Ciana and I had a FaceTime chat this past weekend. I got to see the baby, and she was so chubby that she reminded me of my younger son Jordan when he was born—fat cheeks and a rotund belly. Love it! During our conversation, I asked her what she decided to do with Carl's ashes. She knew how broken I was over his death. She was sensitive enough to ask me if it would upset me if she showed me. I said that I would like to see, since the last vision I had was him being in a cardboard US Postal Service box, and it didn't sit well with me. She brought her iPhone over to her fireplace mantle and showed me a beautiful wooden urn with my brother's name engraved on it—first, middle, and last name. I was so happy to see that he had a proper resting place. The only thing that was upsetting was the birth and death date, especially since March 17th, St. Patrick's Day, would have been my brother's 60th birthday, and it was coming up soon. Again, I tried to stuff this into a place deep down. But it would always come back in the nighttime, when the demons come out.

56

SADNESS

I woke up at 4:30 a.m. thinking, "OK, I'll be ready for my breakfast plans today with my friends." Then I saw last night's wine sitting on my bedside table, and I remembered what today was. Today would have been Carl's 60th birthday. Instead of rolling over and trying to go back to sleep or picking up a book to read, I chugged the wine instead. Since Carl's death, I had been drinking wine at the end of the evening to go to sleep. I couldn't close my eyes like I used to and drift off to sleep because all the images, thoughts, and bad feelings of what happened this year would come into my head. I was self-medicating with wine because, when I closed my eyes, I saw my brother on the ventilator looking like he was peacefully sleeping, and the reality was that he was no longer with us.

I remember sobbing in his hospital room, putting my head on his chest and saying, "Why, why, why? How did this happen?" Of course, Dan was beside me, holding me up as I grieved and cried through this unbearable pain. I ran my hand across Carl's head, so bruised from the fall, with the insane, unrealistic notion that I could somehow magically fix him. My crying came from a place so deep within. I didn't even recognize it myself. Then something really annoying happened. As I was in this moment, staff members, aides, and nurses passing by started to stare and linger, watching me in my deep private moment. I said to Dan, "Pull that curtain closed to give me some privacy with my brother, or I may kill someone today!"

57

A SMALL WINDOW

Today, I was feeling despondent because a friend asked me, "Why can't you just feel happy today and have fun!" That sounded great, and I wished I could just flick the magic, "I had my breasts removed, lost a big part of my mother to dementia, and had my brother die suddenly via a senseless horrific accident" happy button on, but I couldn't.

However, I was continuing on. I was driving and doing what was expected of me, which was more than a lot of people with my burden could possibly handle. I pulled up to my favorite Italian market, which, even when I'm sad, always makes me happy. After making my selections, I went to the cashier, and I heard "Drops of Jupiter," by Train playing on the radio. I don't think anyone in the store heard it except me, but that didn't matter because I was the intended recipient for this song. It was a song that was special to Marianne. We played it in hospice, and it was pivotal during her funeral—and still today for many of us who cherish her and grieve our loss of her.

On the way home, I was thinking of work-related tasks that needed to be tended to, and I was a little behind the eight ball and needed to get to them. I happened to glance up, and the address on a house on this random street that I passed was 311, March 11th, Marianne's birthday. My mood changed, and I became totally in tune to who was guiding me on what I thought was an empty, sad journey, moving to one that opened up to a window of hope. I was now in control of today and what was really meaningful to me.

I find this quote to be very soothing:

> *"Sometimes you just have to hang on and trust that life's storms are carrying you to better shores." – Jane Lee Logan*

58

TIME FOR ANOTHER WEDDING!

More than a year after my mastectomy, I was still experiencing social anxiety, especially when I saw people I hadn't seen since before all this happened. This usually occurred at special events such as weddings.

We were on our way to our friends' Donna and Jim's daughter's wedding, and I felt that uneasy, uncomfortable feeling enveloping me. I've had this before, so I had a pretty good method for handling it: Breathing, self-talk, and sharing my feelings with Dan, the person who has seen me through this entire journey.

We pulled up to the place, and there were a sea of cars waiting to valet park, as well as shuttle buses with people being brought from nearby hotels and beautiful, elegantly dressed people exiting vehicles and entering the building. I said to Dan, "There are plenty of parking spots right over there. Let's just pull in so that later we don't have to wait on the enormous line to get our car." Zoom, and we were in a spot and entering the building.

Because of the social anxiety, I wanted to find our table at the reception, drop my stuff off there, and then find the mojo to face the people I was afraid to encounter because I knew unequivocally that their glances downward at my breasts when we first met were going to make me feel uncomfortable, different, and changed.

We made our way to the stand-alone table where they had place cards identifying where we would be sitting. My anxiety was high because all I wanted to do was grab the card, find our table, place my stuff there, and then push through and get beyond the first encounter with the guests—friends I hadn't seen in quite some time. Unfortunately, there was this old guy —and I'm usually kind and compassionate to old people— blocking off my ability to grab and go. This freaking guy was hovering and consuming the entire place card table, making it impossible for me to scoop up my card, indicating where Mr. & Mrs. Dan Mankes were seated. After a couple of polite gestures, the "Brooklyn" came out of me, and I made my way around him, scooped up our card, handed it to Dan, and off we went to the reception hall to place our stuff at table #3. Done!

We headed to the outdoor bar, and I ordered a glass of wine to take the edge off what I anticipated might be coming up. Ahh ... soothing! That was when I had the opportunity to scan the room and subsequently realize I did not recognize anyone there. Of course, I would recognize my close friends and even the ones I hadn't seen since before my surgery, the ones I was fearful of seeing. I had a good memory, and I remembered Donna and Jim's family from the engagement party, and there was not one face remotely familiar to me. I said to Dan, "I don't see anyone I know here." So, I turned to the bartender and asked, "Is this the DeMarco wedding?"

To which he replied, "Yes, it is."

A few minutes later, my husband was still oblivious to the situation and wanted to make his way over to the hors d'oeuvres they were passing along. I told him to hold up a minute, as I was convinced there was something amiss. I decided to ask someone more official at the front door, "Excuse me, is this the DeMarco wedding?"

He shook his head and told me, "The wedding you're supposed to be attending is across the parking lot in the next building."

I asked him, "Can we bring our drinks?" mostly because I still had social anxiety, and I needed a numbing agent to avoid feeling vulnerable and weak when meeting up with the other guests.

He said, "Sure, why not?" We silently made a walk of shame across the parking lot to the right wedding, carrying our glasses of wine. We entered the venue and immediately met up with people we knew.

This was the perfect way to break through the social anxiety since Rosie Mankes had a zany story to share. The funny thing was that the other wedding had a full bar and hors d'oeuvres, so when we walked in carrying wine, our neighbors and friends were pissed off that they weren't offered wine.

To which I responded, "Sorry, you should've crashed the other wedding!"

59

THINGS I WOULD MISS IF I DIED

I wrote this list on a night in spring 2017 when I was feeling sad about all that had happened to me:

The look of love on my sons' faces. Not the kind of look that comes when I buy them something or do something that makes them happy. The once-in-a-while moment when I genuinely see how much they care about me—a look that they cannot show too often because it might make them somehow seem uncool. But, every so often, it comes through, and, for a few seconds, I feel that connection—and all the sacrifices, compromises, and selfless acts that I made, and only learned how to do by becoming a mother are worth it.

The sun on my face. The warmth, the calm soothing feeling that it brings to my body and soul. Suddenly, all my senses are alive—I hear the birds singing quietly in the background. I sense the trees swaying softly and the sun warming my body, invigorating me and telling me to take it in and feel the moment.

The ocean. There's nothing more powerful and mighty to me than the waves crashing on the surf, one after the other—rumbling, roaring, continuous, yet soothing. Walking in the sand with no predetermined destination in mind, with my feet gently being tickled by the ocean as the waves rush in and out, is so peaceful.

Great sex. Not the obligatory once-or twice-a-week that I feel compelled to do based on an unwritten rule book so that I can stay connected and happily married. What I mean is great sex, the kind that makes my body, mind, and soul get swept away for a few precious moments and forget all the other things going on in my life that, seconds before, needed to be taken care of. It's a moment when I'm fully connected to my husband, and the only thing that matters is how incredible we are feeling. Selfishly, we don't want it to end, and we'd like every encounter to be like this. But it can't because, if it was, it would be less special and memorable.

Love. When I start to love someone, I love how it continues to build, and it becomes bigger and better as the years pass. What makes our heart able to love so many people for so many different reasons and attributes each possess?

Friendships. Not the superficial ones where we say to each other, let's check calendars and get together soon and nothing comes of it because it's empty. But the real friendships, and for me, the women in this group are more like sisters to me. We work on our friendships, building everlasting love, laughter, and celebrations of milestones, especially as we watch our children thrive. We make meaningful plans and live to fulfill our bucket lists, which are tall orders. We cry for each other, feel pain, and our hearts ache and feel joy when each of us experience the ups and downs that life puts before us. I suspect from experience that many upcoming outings on our bucket lists will be filled with laughter and zaniness, which, in and of itself, is a blessing to look forward to.

Dan. The young man who came into my life when I was 19 years old, when I was not even looking for a full-time boyfriend, not to mention a life partner. Someone who could drive an hour to our destination, a wine and cheese place with a solo guitarist playing in the background, hold my hand, gaze into my eyes, and somehow make me know at such a young age that he was the one for me, someone who has seen me through some of my best accomplishments but has also seen me through my darkest days, someone who has not wavered or doubted who I am and what I'm capable of doing. Like my sons, Dan has always said, "You got this!" no matter how hard the obstacle has been. And there have been so many difficult hurdles. Many people have asked me how I survived, how I did not commit suicide during that horrible year. I can't say that, after Carl's death, and the panic of what might come next, it didn't cross my mind. But the, "You got this. You've been to hell and back" pushed me, coupled with the profound, intense love I feel for my children and Dan, that made me want to continue on.

Music. During that horrible year, I turned off the radio because I stopped believing in things that made me happy, and I couldn't fathom singing along to something or concentrating on the lyrics in a song. But music is such an important part of my life, and I mourn the fact that I let it slip away at a time I probably needed it most. I'm not referring to fun music that makes me feel like singing and dancing, or music that just puts a smile on my face. Songs like these are important to me, but what's really important are lyrics that are poetic and tell a story that speaks directly to me, such as "Vienna" or "Summer Highland Falls" from Billy Joel. Since I was in my early teens, these songs have been in my life, running through my mind. They're my "go-to place" when I need solace or just need to reflect on certain private moments.

"Who Knew" by Pink is another song that I selfishly feel was written to describe my relationship and feelings for Marianne, my angel, who is always with me and has been sitting on my shoulder through this entire journey. The number 311, her birthday, comes before me at least once a day, whether it be on an address I pass, on the clock in the car when I glance down to check the time, a cashier's receipt, or countless other times, reminding me that she's here, trying to help me heal.

The sunrise and more importantly the sunset. I'm not an early riser, so it's rare I catch a sunrise. But I'm completely attuned to sunsets, and friends of mine have called Dan and I the "Sunset Chasers" because, when we happen to see a beautiful one, I take a photo of it and share it on Facebook. The colors, the hues, the beauty of how the end of the day easing into the night is captured by the sky is breathtaking, and I marvel at how each time can be different, yet entrancing. Coincidentally, I got up early today, and this morning's sunrise is starting off grey and white, with hints of purple and fiery yellow starting to nudge their way in. Just beautiful.

My babies. Most people might be confused now, thinking that I'm referring to my children. But once our maltese and shih tzu, Nico and Mojo, entered our life, they became our babies. I resisted having pets for many years, as the responsibility of motherhood felt like more than enough of a challenge, but once I opened my heart and our home to these two little boys, WOW! What joy they have brought to us. Yes, there have been challenges, but the unconditional love and the companionship when I've felt so very despondent has been profound. I look into their eyes, and they look back at me, and I see two little guys that rely on my every move, all day, every day, for guidance, love, and sustenance. And what they give back to me when they greet me in the morning with such enthusiasm and affection, and how they snuggle next to me on the couch at night, so content and so connected, is something priceless.

Watching my children thrive. I think of the special women in my life who passed away before their time, and I distinctly remember the looks on their faces when their children shared plans for their future, and they knew that they wouldn't be there to participate in them. My heart ached at these moments. I know this is deep, and perhaps hard to read, but after two cancer struggles, I'm elated to still be sitting here for the time being and able to watch my children grow, learn, push themselves beyond their limits, make plans, and seize the day! I'm in awe of how dedicated they are to their goals, how they have their eyes on the prize and know exactly what they want at such young ages—25 and 22 years old. Additionally, I love that they're warm, gentle, kind young men. Most importantly, I really love hanging out with them, learning about what's important in their lives, having them share their dreams and the fact that they enjoy spending quality time with my husband and me. This is really special, and a beautiful blessing. We did a good job, Dan Mankes! I LOVE YOU!!!

Driving with no predetermined destination in mind. We always have so many places to go and so much to do, but, on a rare occasion, I have an afternoon to myself, and that's when I take off. Sometimes I drive, just to go to scenic places to enjoy the view or take a long walk, especially if it's warm enough to walk on the boardwalk and enjoy the ocean. Other times, I drive and randomly pick places that I used to enjoy going to, but, over time and because of new responsibilities, I don't have the opportunity to visit. What's intriguing and special is that this precious time is not planned out, it's spontaneous, and sort of a surprise, a gift I give to myself because it's something I don't have to do. I'm doing it just because it brings joy and a sense of adventure to me. During that horrible year, among the many restrictions I had, driving was one of them. And, for a period of time, I had to rely on my family and friends to take me places, which made me feel weak and helpless. Once I got the thumbs-up to drive again, I sort of lost my mojo to drive, not locally, but on the Garden State Parkway, because it was a place that I might have to react and respond quickly, and I was very afraid I wouldn't be able to do so. Slowly, I was easing my way back to this wonderful freedom, to go off on journeys with no pre-planned routes or outcomes. Exciting!

My mom, before the dementia. This entry is very painful for so many reasons. When HER mom was diagnosed with dementia, it was her greatest fear that it would happen to her and, subsequently, it's been one of my greatest fears for myself. Before dementia, my mom was my go-to person for so many things—motherhood, cooking tips, advice on life and marriage. Although her marriage sucked, she still had a logical, natural handle and a soothing way to provide guidance.

Even though my mom was forced to leave school before she graduated high school, she was a very smart, practical, no-nonsense, tough-as-nails woman. Most importantly, she was the bond that kept what could have been an insane upbringing normal and stabilized. Our lives as children, as dysfunctional as they were due to my father, could have been so much worse if she had not provided the customary, daily traditional routines to us, coupled with the Italian culture, rituals, and specialness that make me so very proud of my heritage.

I don't know what I would have done if I had not had my mother by my side when I became a mother because she taught and guided me through all I needed to learn and know how to do it. I marvel at the fact that it was 28 years before that she had to do this with me, her youngest, yet she knew instinctively how to do it and did it seamlessly and effortlessly, which gave me the confidence to do it myself.

I learned the foundation of family from her. I learned that, when someone enters our kitchen, my kitchen, to sit down and eat a meal, that you stop and sit with them because it's important to spend a few moments connecting with the special people in your life, especially as they take a break to enjoy food—another thing that is extremely important in Italian culture.

I learned to be fair but tough. No free passes. My mom taught me, which in turn instilled in me the need to teach my kids, that you and only you are accountable for your own actions. If something bad goes down, and you're involved in it, own it, learn from it, and make sure you're a better person the next time a similar situation presents itself. She also made me the type of mother who didn't run to bail my kids out of situations. Instead, I've made them figure out how to solve their own problems—because, at the end of the day, they were their problems, and it was not my place to get involved. Of course, there was always the guidance and coaching that was provided by her and subsequently by me to my children, but when it came time to face the world, she taught me that it wasn't my job to "fix it" for my kids. I gave them the tools to make it right, but it was up to them to do it themselves.

I think one of the most important lessons she taught me was to not give up on my dreams. I wanted to go to college and be the first in my family to attend for four consecutive years and graduate. Somewhere along the line, I got sidetracked by my friends, who had gone straight from high school into jobs, and I was attracted to the money they were making. I can distinctly remember standing by the sink, washing dishes (because we didn't have a dishwasher and the women in the house cleaned up after dinner, while the men went off to watch TV), saying to my mother, "I'm thinking of dropping out of Pace University and going to work because my friends are making $150.00 a week." Back in 1982, that seemed like a lot of money. I remember my mother, she stopped and paused, having had three children before me drop out of college, and said, "No, you're going to finish what you started." Plain and simple. No more explanation. Since then, I've thanked her personally and silently on countless occasions that she pushed me to continue on.

So, up until five years ago, I had my mom, whole and complete, and I spent lots of time giving back to her by taking over where she left off, hosting the family gatherings and being the glue that kept us together. She loved showing me off, her daughter, and shared on numerous occasions, and still today, that I was the one who took over the reins.

Unfortunately, the dementia seeped in, and some digestive issues also became a part of her life, which made it difficult for us to maintain the type of life that I had hoped for in her golden years. I mourn every day the restrictions I have with her, and all that we could do together if the limitations didn't exist.

But I have my mom here with me today, living in an assisted living facility about 10 minutes away from my house, and I think we're turning a corner. She has a regularly scheduled poker game, and she has a posse of friends. They accept the fact she repeats things every 30 seconds. They have a social hour at 4:00 p.m. every day, where they serve wine and engage her with daily activities. Slowly, she's settling in. We're no longer in a gigantic struggle with her, fighting us to leave and return to Brooklyn. The battle is still there, but now it comes and goes. It's not constant.

On a completely different note, and getting back to closing the loop on what I would miss if I died, I told Dan if I ever found out that I was terminally ill and nothing else could be done for me, I needed a hall pass from him. Before I sign up for the Death with Dignity Act, also known as the Assisted Suicide Act, I want to have the following: lots of vodka, a brownie sundae, and a good amount of time with a very well endowed, highly skilled, 30-year-old muscular porn star named Thor, in no particular order, but hopefully all in the same week! Oh, and perhaps a lobster tail and a petit filet mignon!

60

MEDITATION

I had started sleeping with a guy named Andy. He whispered into my ear every night, and his voice was incredibly soothing. Suddenly and miraculously, I was falling asleep, sleeping through the night and not drinking wine to do so.

No, I wasn't cheating on my husband. My therapist recommended I investigate a meditation app, so, after our session, I came home and Googled it. Not getting all the information I needed, I called the customer service number. I explained my situation, that I was having trouble sleeping and wanted to explore meditation vs. wine as a way of naturally falling asleep.

"We have several options with this package," the rep said. "There are daily meditations, ones for anxiety, stress, and anger, and we have one dedicated to sleep." I was sold and bought the package on the spot.

Back to Andy: He was the narrator of each meditation track on Headspace, so, every night, for the past month, I went to bed, and put my earbuds in. Then Andy softly spoke to me with his "oh-so-soothing voice," and I drifted off to sleep. It took a bit of time before it worked, but slowly I was beginning to sleep without drinking wine. This, among some other significant things I had chosen to do to heal, were powerful steps, necessary for helping me find my way back to myself again.

61

PONDERING

For a little while, can't I just live and stop trying to accomplish something or, better yet, cease in trying to get through a struggle? Suddenly, perhaps because of the meditation, I was seeing the world through a different lens, and I was laughing, playing music, flirting with my husband, appreciating the beauty of the world, and, most importantly, just looking at beautiful moments with my family. I was taking the time to freeze the frame and really feel the intensity and specialness of precious encounters with the people I so deeply love.

It had been a long time since any of this had happened for me, so I wanted to breathe it in, live it, and not have my head cluttered, thinking of the things that have happened to me because it depleted me of the joy I was feeling—and I was left, the next day, feeling exhausted. For now, I wanted to take the enormous pressure I felt every day away for a while, enjoy the day, just a couple of days, maybe more, without having to think of another task I needed to do. Sometimes, when running through all the things that have happened to me, I felt like I was going to implode. I wanted to take my head off of my body so I didn't have to think about it, or how I got there, or, more importantly, why all of this happened to me.

My therapist said that not only do I need to write about my feelings during these times but also focus on the positive things in my life, the joys such as my children, Dan, the special family members, and friends, to help me get through this.

62

LET IT BE

I woke up at 3:30 a.m. and needed to come downstairs to write this:

"Let It Be." Paul McCartney wrote this song, and it didn't really take on a significant meaning in my life until I met Marianne—and especially until she became ill and started dying. "Let It Be." What does that mean? Is it the acceptance of things you can't control? Is it giving things up to your higher power, if you've connected to one, to take the reins and guide you through difficult times?

In the present moment, whenever I heard this song, I knew my very close friend who passed way before her time was telling me from beyond to let things happen the way they were meant to unfold. She was telling me to not try to manipulate and manage what I thought I had control of because, in reality, I didn't have control of many of the things coming up in my future. In the past, I learned this the hard way, when I incessantly worried and obsessed about things that were ahead of me and how I was going to fix them. It took time and lots of work, but then I realized that these things only took up space in my head, and, ultimately, I had no control of the outcome. Sure, I had the power to make informed decisions to guide me toward the path I wanted to be on, but I couldn't completely control where things netted out.

So, back to "Let It Be." Here was a song that used to be so painful for me to hear because it reminded me of Marianne's illness and death. This song was so special to her, and, to commemorate her life, it was played during her wake and church service. As the years passed, I have evolved, and I now understand a different meaningful side of this song, particularly as I have experienced my own significant health and life issues. Currently, I view "Let It Be" as a guide, a rule book for the day-to-day events we experience: the joys, disappointments, and lessons we learn, particularly moments when we need to rise up—most times unexpectedly—and be more than we imagine ourselves capable of being.

Unfortunately, some days were just difficult ones, plain and simple, and I wished they would go away. I couldn't wait to go to sleep and pray that tomorrow would be a bit better. So, one place to turn was to "Let It Be!"

What's interesting is the juxtaposition of what this song can be to me vs. so many others. That's the beauty of what music is for us. A way of listening to a song you've connected with and interpreting and ingraining it within your life so that it's etched into your soul, your inner core. It helps you feel settled, soothed, and inspired. On the opposite side of the spectrum, for others perhaps, it's just a song, a random piece of music to sing along to on the radio. Either way, if you find the lyrics to a particular song to be profound, timeless, and moving, and they help you during a difficult journey, this can be very powerful, so let it bring you comfort. Today and every day I feel grateful for many things—to have had an intimate, special friendship with Marianne, for her husband and her children, and the personal growth I have started to experience during this journey that's now allowing me to "Let It Be."

63

ANOTHER STEP FORWARD

Her name was Sherry, and she was a new life coaching client. She called me, terrified, because she was just diagnosed with breast cancer, and her surgeon and oncologist recommended she have a mastectomy. She was searching the web and came across one of my blogs in which I share parts of my journey. She told me, after reading my blog, that she immediately felt a connection to me and wanted to know if I could help her. Of course, I wanted to help her because I know the exact place that she was sitting in—so fearful, full of questions, afraid, and not really sure where to go to find answers. The medical questions were for the doctors, but the personal ones? Who do you turn to for these?

We started working together, and she continued as a client well over a year after her diagnosis. She said I was one of the only blessings that came from this. This made me proud of my choice to do this work as well as the motivational speaking, and, truth be told, she was a blessing to me as well!

Speaking of which, I started practicing gratitude every day. I also began wearing a bracelet called a Blessings Bracelet. It had four beads on it, and, every day, I acknowledged four blessing in my life, one for each bead. This started my morning off feeling thankful for the gifts I had in front of me, and it cast out to the rest of my day, creating positivity for what I had now and hope for what lay ahead of me.

∼

I find this quote to be very soothing:

> *"You can't go back and change the beginning, but you can start where you are and change the ending." – C. S. Lewis*

64

A SOBERING SUNRISE

As I mentioned earlier, until I found meditation and my new best friend Andy, I had been self-medicating with wine to fall asleep because I couldn't close my eyes without thinking of all the fearful things I pushed out of my head during the day. During the darkness and quiet of night, when I was alone with my thoughts, it was too hard to deal with my struggles, disappointments, and sadness unless I numbed them with wine. I couldn't get the image of Carl out of my head when he was clinically dead, his mind gone and his body a shell of who he once was. He was kept alive so we could hold him, mourn, and grieve this inconceivable loss. This, coupled with the post-traumatic stress of having my breasts removed, trying to create a new normal with that, and the unbelievably difficult transition of moving my mom from Brooklyn to an assisted living facility became my nighttime demons. My sleep each night was interrupted as I tossed and turned, trying to find a way to relax my body, feel tranquility, and rest.

The power and gift that meditation has given me is that it allows me to clear my mind, focus on my breathing, and find inner peace and a calmness that has not existed since before this journey began. I was immensely grateful to Andy from Headspace for teaching me this.

Most mornings before I found meditation were somewhat fuzzy, and I had a dull headache. This morning, I was experiencing a sobering, serene sunrise, one that was not marred by the twisted, tormented sleep I had felt over the past year. This morning, I had clarity, purpose, hopefulness, and peace as I watched the light break through the darkness, present its beautiful colors, and start a new day.

65

THE NOTE

*L*ast night, I took out our wedding album to look at the photos. On June 5th, Dan and I would celebrate our 30th Wedding Anniversary. Wow! 30 years. I couldn't say it had been easy—mostly good, but there were a lot of curveballs that neither of us expected or anticipated. The best blessings had been the boys, our sons, Greg and Jordan. As I perused the pictures, I looked closely at Dan and my 29- and 24-year-old faces to really see how much we'd changed. As I glanced at the group family photos, I noticed how many people were no longer with us. This made me sad.

I thought again about our vows, "For better or worse, in sickness or health, 'til death do us part." We had worked very hard to continue to exist as Daniel and Rosemarie, the couple married on that breezy, sunny afternoon in June.

Suddenly, a folded piece of paper fell out of the wedding album onto the floor. I opened it up, and my eyes widened as I realized what it was. It was the note that Marianne's mother wrote and included in the gift box for my 40th birthday back in 2004. I reminisced about that moment; the note inside the box was from her mom because Marianne passed away three weeks before the surprise birthday party Dan threw for me and, of course, was not able to write it. I had not discovered this note until last year. I must have tucked it into our wedding album when I found it. Taking it in my hands, I read the words out loud, "Now, don't be sad, Rosie. Marianne wants you to find your joy and run with it!"

Tears streamed down my face. It was a little over two years since my mastectomy, and approximately a year-and-a-half since Carl passed on. My dear friend, who had been with me this entire journey, had just sent me another "wink" or message from beyond. Perhaps it was time to heed this advice—to try not to be sad and start to *Find my joy and run with it.*

66

UPDATE

I had begun life coaching, starting motivational speaking, and it felt great to do what I set out to do —to take my experiences and the training and do something purposeful with it. Isn't that why I was still here? To use what I learned in the trenches of my battle-scarred life to help others. This was a powerful and exciting idea.

I was reading a couple of self-help, inspirational blogs. I won't get into specific details, but essentially they shared that, if you write your intentions for what you want to do and work on them every day, you can achieve your goals and be who you want to be, have the life you aspire to have, and be happy.

I was willing to take a shot at this because I had spent so much time being unhappy that I thought it was time to turn things upside down and work toward a world where I was thriving, helping others, and not just limping through life surviving.

I was also utilizing the visualization techniques I used during the time I was experiencing social anxiety, but not for dealing with or overcoming negative, fearful experiences but, instead, creating positive ones. I began to creatively visualize "who I really am" and how I can help my clients and audience to understand that there can be life, a very good life, one filled with gratitude and positivity, after experiencing adversity.

∽

I find this quote to be very soothing:

> *"Sometimes you have to let go of the picture of what you thought life would be like and learn to find joy in the story you are actually living." – Rachel Marie Martin*

67

FLIGHT TIME

We flew to Atlanta today for work. Both Dan and I had business in the area, so we decided to make a little work/vacation out of it. The plane took off, and, after about 15 minutes, I started to hear a strange noise. A female flight attendant happened to walk by just around that time, so I turned to her and asked, "Excuse me, what's that noise?"

She replied, "You know, I've never heard that before."

Then she took off to attend to other matters. I looked at Dan and said, "What the fuck? What about that training they have where they're supposed to say, 'Oh, don't worry. Flying is the safest mode of travel. You're more likely to have an accident while driving or in your bathtub.'"

She came back a couple of minutes later and sensed that I still looked apprehensive about the strange noise, so she said, "Well, you're here now, so if there's anything wrong with the plane, there's nothing you can do about it!"

I shook my head in disbelief. She asked if we wanted drinks, "just in case there's more to the noise than we would hope for."

I responded, "Bring it on!" In this case, I thought a little wine might be required.

6 8

VISITING WITH MOM

After I came back from Atlanta, I visited my mom and showed her pictures of her great Granddaughter Maea. Her face always lit up with such joy when she saw our newest addition to the family. This made me smile, seeing my mom happy.

She asked me if I spoke to Carl, and whether he'd been to Colorado to see the baby. I responded, "Yes, he was there a couple of weeks ago and is thrilled to be a grandfather." My heart sunk a bit, telling this lie that I knew must be told, but I held my composure.

My mom looked at me and said, "You look so tired. I know something is wrong, and you're not telling me. I can see it in your face."

Now it was game time. I HAD to pull this off. I responded, "Yes, Mom, I'm tired. I've been working very hard lately. There's nothing wrong, but, unfortunately, I have to leave to get back to work." I then kissed her goodbye, waved to her friends, and left the building. I sat in my car and cried. I stayed there for about 10 minutes until I was able to drive and focus, so I could make my way home. This was our life now. We made the decision to keep Carl alive to protect her, and we must live with it.

My friend Geri told me recently, "You must be going out of your mind, having to lie as you do and keep this secret from your mom. You can't even grieve Carl's death because you're always pretending he's still here for her sake." This was true, but the alternative of telling her would have had devastating consequences, and I, personally, was not going to allow that to happen.

I hit the ignition button to turn the car on to head home, and the song playing on the radio was "Let It Be." My friend Marianne was telling me what I needed to do.

69

WHEN I BEGAN TO TURN THE CORNER

Something I'd like to share with you: Prior to this very challenging time in my life, I always thought "big picture." If I could just do "this one big thing, I could fix my problem." However, I've learned during this journey that it would not be one big thing that would help me move from adversity to emotional wellness; instead, it would be a series of small things that, when brought together, would create change.

Before I started thinking about integrating the below ideas into my life, I knew I was not going to be able to do them collectively all at once. As such, I decided to list the things that were important to me, things I thought would help me to heal and turn them into meaningful, action-oriented affirmations. These are strong, positive, significant changes and goals I wanted to incorporate into my life. I worked on each of these separately, over and over in my head. As time went by, and I became stronger and believed in the importance of each, I transitioned them from things I wanted to do, to things that I assimilated into my day-to-day life. Exciting and powerful! Here's how it happened:

I came home one night and said to myself, "I don't know how much time I have left, plain and simple. I tested positive for four cancer genes and I had already migrated through two cancer journeys. Spending my time being sad was just taking days and joy away from me when I had so much of it stolen already." Here's what I mapped out and started to implement:

I decided that, every morning, I would greet my dogs, Nico and Mojo, in the same manner that they greet me. I would give them a *proper hello*, not just a quick pat on the head, but a genuine *proper hello*. So now, every morning, when I come down the stairs, I would sit on the floor and give them the same level of attention that they give to me, hugging, kissing them, and saying good morning. It felt great because they were so happy and excited to see me that it helped me frame out the rest of my day and the choices I could make as to how it would go.

I'd also been looking at the sky differently. I now noticed all the colors, the cloud formations, the way the sun etches its way in. More importantly, I started to understand what was beyond and within that sky, how significant it was to cast my eyes on it and recognize the beauty, mystery, and the entrancing details. Sometimes, I looked and had to turn my eyes away because it was too much to take in at once. This is probably too deep and far-fetched for some, but this was how I felt! When I looked at the sky, particularly when rays of sun pierced the clouds, streaming light down toward us, I knew that this was our loved ones who had passed, showing us that they were with us, sharing their presence so that we could feel them and not only remember them for when they were here, but feel joy in knowing that they were still with us—a gentle, beautiful reminder.

I started to live in the present moment. This was one of the by-products and benefits of meditating. I spent so much FUCKING time worrying, obsessing, plotting, planning, and scheming about how things would turn out with my mother, my health issues, and so many countless things through the past couple of years. At some point, I started reading a book called *Jesus Calling* and decided I would commit to reading two pages each day. This book, along with my very skilled, unbelievably awesome therapist, taught me to stay present and that it was counterproductive to try to plan and control the future. Sure, you could work and make plans for things you would like to occur, but sometimes, the best place to be was exactly where your feet were planted at the moment. These were not my words, but my therapists'—insight that was so relevant and meaningful to me.

It took a bit of time for me to reconnect with my higher power, but I now knew that one existed and was guiding me to the decisions and places I needed to be so that I no longer felt it was necessary to map the path on my own. The book *Jesus Calling* was also helping me realize that I had to stop trying to control my world because there was absolutely no way I could do so, yet there was, according to what I now believed, a plan for me that would lead me to what I wanted. Although it may take a while, I hoped to have the time to find it and see it to fruition. I felt that I had valuable information, insight, and guidance to give to others, but my fear was that I would run out of time before I was able to do so. Yet I was inspired. As Billy Joel said, in yet another of my favorite songs, I was "Keeping the Faith."

I also started practicing daily meditation, which was a total game changer! It taught me there was a place so deep inside of me that I didn't know existed, a place that was so peaceful and serene. Anyone who knew me well knew that I had a busy brain that was always on overdrive, but the fact that I had found my way to this profound level of connectivity beyond what I ever expected was so very powerful and wonderful. It brought life back to me, a person who thought at one point that I no longer had a reason to exist. After my meditations with Andy from Headspace, I became acutely aware of all life's offerings, the beauty, the power of something beyond what I'd ever known, and its ability to restore me to a thriving person who was more alive than ever before. This was so very exciting.

I also incorporated exercise back into my life—something so simple, yet so disappointing and debilitating if it's taken away from you. I had been using exercise as a release for my tension since I was a young teenager. When I had my surgery, however, I had to give up my high-powered workout classes and go into "down-time mode." As a compromise, I started to walk miles and miles, and I created the Positano to keep myself fit and sane. Yet there was something missing —the dancing, jumping, lunges, squats, and other heart-pumping moves that made me feel alive and young. When I say "young," I mean that I work out like an 18-year-old when I feel good and have the opportunity to do so. But that went away for over two years, and now it was back. AWESOME!!!

The first year I had to forgo exercise was for practical, restrictive, and recovery reasons, following the mastectomy and then the reconstructive surgery. The second year was because I was so despondent over Carl's death, and my anxiety was through the roof. I didn't have the confidence to walk into a workout class and participate.

Two years after my surgical journey, however, I woke up one day and decided I didn't care who was in the work out class. I didn't need to go with a friend. I just needed to go for me. And that was exactly what I did. I started taking Zumba classes again. I went in tentatively, the first couple of times of course, but, over time, I built up the confidence to work out to my level and boom, boom, boom—my heart was racing, and I felt alive and happy. I was "in the moment, feeling the music" and I had the biggest smile on my face. I was back doing what I loved, dancing, sweating, and singing along to my favorite Zumba songs and it felt amazing!

To some, this may not be important or resonate with you, and, to others, you may not have the ability to do this because of health issues or the situation you're in, but, for me, I needed this back. I was thankful for the way it helped me turn the corner during one of the most difficult times in my life.

I also became more attuned to simple acts of kindness. I had always been a kind person, but now I wanted to be better than I was before and more conscious and attuned to anyone who might need a hand, my ear, or my time. I wanted to be the best version of myself, one who distinctly understood when a friend, family member, or stranger was lonely, fearful, unsure, or just needed something basic—to stop what I was doing and throw myself into their world to provide guidance and support.

I spent the better part of the last couple of years worrying and obsessing about my own problems and the ultimate outcome of them, while those around me tried to help by providing guidance, sometimes fumbling and falling because they simply didn't know what to do to help get me out of the enormous hole I had spiraled into. With their help (especially Dan's, who has had to ride the Rosie Mankes Crazy Train through this whole experience), lots of therapy, and all of the above-mentioned learning experiences, I was able to start actively working and focusing on others—to pay it forward as they say—and bring light, insight, guidance, comfort, and peace into the world of those currently living with anxiety and uncertainty.

70

PRIVATE DANCE LESSONS WITH DAN

I was so terrified when I learned that I had breast cancer, that I needed a double mastectomy. Then I became incredibly sad and riddled with anxiety after Carl passed. In my mind, 2016 was going to be the year that Dan and I took dance lessons, particularly salsa and bachata, because I wanted to know how to dance to my favorite music with my husband. Then everything fell apart, and I went into survival mode, and dancing became the farthest thing from my mind. It took two years, but we finally enrolled in private lessons recently, and I was super excited that we were doing this together as a couple.

To be my rock during the last couple of years, Dan became stoic and methodical. His willingness to take over at a time I was incapable of functioning at full capacity saved me, but somewhere he lost his ability to have fun and be relaxed. I too have experienced this, but I was now ready to integrate this back into our lives.

We had our first lesson with JJ, a 28-year-old Latino man with a beautiful smile and an easygoing manner. He was also a great dancer, naturally. I jokingly told Dan that I would rather go out dancing with him because he was a fantastic lead and made me look good when we danced together.

JJ was always patient with us. He laughed along with us when we messed up on our steps, and I was beginning to see a playful side of Dan I hadn't seen in so very long. When you're taught to dance together, the instructor encourages you to look into each other's eyes. Whether this is for intimate reasons or just so that the female dancer can pick up on cues that her male lead is going to move to another step, I don't know. But there was something very sexy and sensual about looking into my husband's eyes as we moved across the dance floor. Sometimes I saw the 24-year-old man looking at me the way he did when we first met, or the man looking into my eyes when we exchanged our wedding vows. Other times, I saw the man holding my hand and coaching me as I pushed and brought our babies into the world—or another moment I would never forget, the man waiting for me, with such compassion and tenderness, to be brought into my hospital room after my double mastectomy. All of these times, I saw the love in his eyes, which made me love him more and feel blessed that God gave him to me because I needed him, love him, and could not have made it through my screwed-up journey if he wasn't next to me all this time, helping me to get up, show up, and make it through each day.

71

SNEAKERS

Prior to the surgery, one of my mastectomy friends suggested I go to the store and buy slip-on laceless sneakers because it would be difficult to bend over to tie my shoes after the procedure. My friend Maribel and I decided to go to the mall, and we stumbled upon Skechers. Surprisingly, they had a large selection, and I easily found a pair I liked. I was amazed at how comfortable and cushioned they were and wondered to myself why I never bought a pair before. I guess it was because I usually wore shoes on a day-to-day basis and only used sneakers for workouts.

    Throughout my breast cancer journey, I wore these sneakers almost every day, and, when the weather was nice, Dan and I walked miles and miles as a means of exercise and stress relief. I must have logged thousands of miles wearing these sneakers walking on the boardwalk at all our favorite towns along the Jersey Shore. In the early days of my recovery, I needed to hold onto Dan's arm to steady myself as we walked, as I was incapable of walking unassisted. As I built up my strength over time, he was the one trying to catch up to me as I took long strides, feeling a sense of independence, power, and freedom from my restrictions.

Two years later, I looked down at the sneakers and saw holes in the top, where my big toe was peeking through. I took this as a sign that it was finally time to retire these sneakers. They had served their purpose, but they needed to go. Being the ritualistic person I am, I decided I wanted to burn them as another means of walking away, so-to-speak, from that chapter in my life and move onto a healthier and happier time. So that was what we did. Last night, we put the sneakers into a garbage can, threw some lighter fluid on them, and watched them burn until they no longer existed. I didn't know if burning rubber-based products was legal, but frankly I didn't care.

While these sneakers helped me get through my journey, it was cathartic to see them go. This was just another way of moving toward healing and stepping it up (pun intended), escalating my exercise regimen back to the level of intensity I was accustomed to, prior to when the restrictions and limitations were placed upon me during breast cancer, which at the time made me so unhappy. Onward!

72

PUBLIC SPEAKING TRAINING

When I decided I wanted to be a motivational speaker, I was still struggling with anxiety and was so worried that I might not be able to speak publicly to large groups of people. I jokingly told Dan, "I really want to be able to share my story and how I've been working through my struggles, but I have one problem."

"What's that?" he replied.

I responded, "I'm afraid of the audience."

Dan kissed my hand and said, "Just be you! Everyone will love you and what you have to say." This was very sweet coming from my husband, but was it true and would I have the moxie to get up in front of hundreds of people—or more—to share my story and what I had learned?

Two people recommended that I take a public speaking course. One was the founder of the current company I had been consulting for the past six years. I asked her months ago, "You seem to be very comfortable speaking publicly. I have a hard time with it, my heart hammers, and I worry and obsess before I have to make the speech. I end up pulling it off, but it takes a lot out of me. Any suggestions?"

She said, "Why don't you consider taking a public speaking course. I haven't done it personally, but I've heard wonderful things about them." By definition, public speaking training is a laboratory for people from two different groups, those who want to hone and improve their public speaking skills and those who want to speak publicly because they feel they have an important message to share but are afraid to do so. I was definitely in the second group!

The other person to mention it to me was my therapist. She said she had a patient who had a high-level job that required him to give speeches, which he had done for some time without a problem, but, somewhere along the way, something went wrong. He started to pass out when he spoke publicly, so he went to a public speaking course to work on and eventually fix his problems.

I mentioned and explained what this was to Dan, and he said he was also interested in going, as it could potentially help him promote and grow his business. Due to weather issues or other commitments, it took us some time to attend a meeting, but, last night, we finally made it to one.

I hate when you read info on a website, and they say things like, "Don't worry, as our guest, you will not be asked to say anything or participate" and then you arrive, and the greeter says, "Hi, I'm Nancy. We're so happy that you're here tonight! We want you to sit back and relax and enjoy the meeting, but, when we start, we'd like you to stand up and introduce yourself. Tell us where you're from, what you do, and why you're interested in public speaking training."

Ugh! I just wanted to sit there and listen and observe. Plus, we arrived exactly at the meeting start time due to traffic. I didn't have time to pee, and they put us at the front of the room so I couldn't quietly exit while someone was giving a speech to relieve myself.

When they called my name to ask me to share my story, I told them my name, where I was from, and I said that I was a life coach and an aspiring motivational speaker. Unfortunately, I went on to explain that I had anxiety and had been, for most of my life, afraid of speaking in front of large groups, which didn't bode well for motivational speakers who want to appeal to large audiences.

The members were so warm and encouraging. One guy named Joe said to me, "Don't worry. We all started where you are now. What's important is that you get outside of your comfort zone, and what better way to do that than with a group of people with the same goals as you." Pretty good insight. Dan and I signed up and committed to doing the work required, with his objective being to grow his business and mine to share my story, learnings, and techniques for healing with a broader audience.

73

THE RAINBOW ROOM

Noreen and her husband asked some of our close friends if we wanted to attend a fancy event at the Rainbow Room in New York City. This was an opportunity to go out, literally, for a night on the town, dress up, dance, and have a great meal and fun with friends we've known for close to 20 years. I told her that Dan and I were definitely "in," and it turned out we had a total of six couples attending.

As we always do when we're getting together for a formal affair, Noreen, Maribel, and I spent the week before brainstorming what we would be wearing—from the dress to the shoes to the purses to the jewelry—until we were satisfied that we'd all look great. This was especially true following my mastectomy. It was so important to them, along with Annie, Geri, and Lori, that I looked my very best when I went out with Dan for a special occasion. If I didn't have something in my closet that they felt would work, they would come over with dresses from theirs, and we would have what is commonly known among us now as "A Fashion Show." I would try on dresses until we all agreed on the perfect one for the upcoming event. This was yet another reason I felt so blessed that these beautiful women were in my life.

The Rainbow Room has been a staple in New York City since 1934. Suffering from a decline in business following the financial crisis of 2007–2008, the Rainbow Room closed in 2009. The restaurant reopened in 2014, following a renovation. Most evenings, the Rainbow Room was reserved for private events and parties, but, on Monday evenings, it was open to the public.

When we arrived, I admired how beautiful it was, the ornate elegance of the room and the revolving dance floor, which had been a part of this venue since it opened. We all took our seats and ordered drinks. I vividly remember watching the people dancing. These were not everyday folks; these couples had learned how to dance professionally, and they glided with ease and confidence across the floor. It made me smile and think about the lessons that Dan and I were now taking.

After ordering dinner, Noreen said she needed to use the ladies' room and asked if anyone else needed to as well. Lori and I joined her, and we headed out of the room. After finishing up, as we were making our way back to the table, something crazy and funny came into my head.

I looked at Noreen, out of the blue, and said, "Do you think anyone at the table would notice if we swapped dresses?" Most normal people would look at me like I was insane, but, for almost 20 years, Noreen has been the Ethel to my Lucy when something like this pops into my warped brain. Noreen stopped short, dead in her tracks, looked at me and said, "Let's do it!" We made an about-face, heading back to the lady's room, with Lori following us, shaking her head, thinking we were crazy.

We picked two stalls opposite each other, took off our respective dresses—mine was sleeveless, and hers had a ¾-length sleeve—and Lori made the swap. The attendant in the bathroom did not know what to do or say. She just stood there with her mouth open as we laughed and giggled about what we were doing.

After finishing, we took a selfie of ourselves in our new attire and posted it on Facebook. We had taken photos in our original dresses when we first arrived and wanted to see if anyone at home would notice. Then we headed back to the table, holding onto each other, and laughing like children. When we got to the door leading into the room, we took a moment to compose ourselves so that we could casually and nonchalantly return to our seats and see if there would be any reaction.

Dan and Noreen's husband stood when we returned to pull our chairs out like perfect gentlemen, which was apropos for an elegant evening such as this. We sat down and sipped our cocktails. Within two minutes of sitting, Maribel looked at us and said, "Oh my God, I can't believe what you two crazy ladies just did."

We tried to pull it off, looking at her like she was the crazy one, saying, "I have no idea what you're talking about."

"You two changed dresses!" she said. The men at the table were clueless, especially Dan and Noreen's husband, because they probably hadn't even noticed what we were originally wearing when we left the house for the evening.

We tried to mess with everyone at the table for a bit longer. Noreen said, "What are you talking about? I bought this dress last week!" After a little while, we fessed up, and everyone at the table was laughing and telling us how crazy we were. Of course, they all knew that this scheme came from me, with Noreen following along, having known us for so many years. I glanced at my phone and saw that there was a comment on Facebook. Our friend, Geri, sitting at home in New Jersey, posted, "WTF, dress swapping!!!" I showed it to Noreen, and she and I looked at each other and said, "Damn, she's good!"

Noreen hugged me because she knew all of the sadness and suffering I had been through, and, prior to the last couple of years, how many zany things I had put her up to when my life was simpler and happier. She raised her glass and said to everyone at the table, "Cheers, I got my Rosie back!!!" Everyone clinked glasses, and it felt so good to be surrounded by my wonderful friends, being present, in the moment and being silly again.

74

LIFE COACHING

At this point, my business was really starting to come together. The young woman I hired to be my social media guru was posting amazing content on Facebook and Instagram. I was getting clients and doing exactly what I intended to do: help people struggling with something, identify where they are now, find out what is holding them back, make a plan and ultimately a commitment regarding what they need to do to move in a positive direction.

I was so at ease and comfortable in this space because of all the battle scars I had endured. I instinctively knew this because I spent so much time in the trenches myself. I knew the right questions to ask, how to make people accountable and responsible. I worked closely with my clients to help them to create actionable goals and plans that were workable and suitable for their current situation.

Business was good in my local community, but, as I've said before, after encountering lung and breast cancer and testing positive for three more mutations through genetic testing, I wanted to share my story beyond New Jersey. I worked with my social media guru this weekend, trying to kick this off. It was so exciting and empowering to be taking my adversity and turning it into meaningful, positive messages and learnings, as well as broadening my audience to, dare I say, a national level!

75

MINDFULNESS

Andy from Headspace has taught me so much about meditation. A couple of months ago, I made a commitment to meditate twice a day, once mid-afternoon, and then again at bedtime as a means of going to sleep naturally without drinking wine.

Perhaps the most exciting thing I learned during this meditation journey is the practice of incorporating mindfulness into my day-to-day life, by staying in the present moment. I also discovered the difference between meditation and mindfulness and, how when both are combined, they have helped me to make profound, meaningful changes. On a personal level, meditation allows me to experience a deep connectivity within my mind, body, and soul, which creates a greater sense of calm, clarity, and focus. Mindfulness connects me to everything in my present life, so that I can acknowledge and rejoice in the gifts that are right in front of me.

I recently began reading a book by Dan Harris, *Ten Percent*

Happier, and it was inspiring to see how meditation, being present and mindful, has transformed his busy brain into one that could find peace and balance in, as my therapist has said to me countless times, staying exactly where your feet are planted at the moment.

Prior to integrating meditation and mindfulness into my life, I was always thinking ahead, planning and plotting what would happen next, or, worse yet, worrying whether I made the right decision yesterday or how I might try to fix some future problem. I was not HERE! I was not present.

My BFFs and I went to see Pink in concert recently, which was awesome, and perhaps one of the best shows I'd ever seen. This was a big statement, coming from me, as my friends and I had a tall bucket list and had seen many shows together.

The morning of the concert, I started thinking about past shows and things I might have been doing during the performance. Part of the time I was in the moment, but, other times, I was taking photos or videos and posting them on Facebook as they occurred. I would check my phone several times to see how many "Likes" or "Comments" I received. Toward the end of the concert, I started scanning the crowd and planning our exit strategy so that we could get out of the venue as quickly as possible. My mind was always busy doing other things; I was not present.

None of this occurred during Pink's recent performance. I stayed completely in the moment, danced, and sang along to her songs with my friends. She rocked it, and I was there, taking it all in. I was totally invested and committed to this special experience, and it felt awesome!

I took one short video of her singing a portion of one of my favorite songs, "Who Knew" as a tribute to Marianne, and, as I always do when I hear this, I looked up to heaven when Pink sung the last verse of the song and sang it to my friend, especially the words, "the last kiss, I'll cherish until we meet again."

Speaking of who knew, who would have imagined that finding mindfulness would be so cathartic! I began sharing how it has helped transform me with my clients and audience—those interested in finding tranquility and harmony within themselves. Whenever I found myself drifting or worrying, I would pull myself back to where I was and pay attention to the blessings and special moments that were right in front of me. I acknowledged and appreciated them. This was powerful stuff.

I had dinner last night with a friend I'd known most of my life. We sat for three hours, laughing and reminiscing about the funny things that had happened through the years. Like myself, she had some difficult challenges. She said something to me that made me pause and think. She said, "You know, Rosie, I'm very happy with my life now."

It hadn't occurred to me for quite some time to think of this for myself, but then, in that moment, while she explained more about why she was happy, I evaluated how I felt. I smiled and said, "Me too! I'm happy with my life now."

Something I'd like to share with you: When I started meditating with Andy and downloaded the app, a prompt asked if I would like to receive daily inspirational messages from him, and I checked the Yes box. I just looked down at my phone to check the time, and there was a message from him. It said, "Have you noticed what's around you at the moment?" Wow, what timing Andy! You just can't make this shit up.

JUNE 5TH, 2018

I opened the small jewelry box I received many years ago. It had aged, just like we all have. It was no longer pristine looking, and it had become a bit tarnished. It had tinges of yellow on it, but that didn't matter because what it contained was what was important to me. I picked up each earring and put them into my ears. They were the pearl earrings that Marianne gave to me 14 years ago for my 40th birthday, the year she passed away. I wanted to honor her on this day, my 30th wedding anniversary, because she had been my angel through this entire journey, guiding and sending me messages to not give up and keep moving forward, even when I thought I didn't have anything left inside of me.

Thirty years ago today, I married my husband Dan, and tonight we would renew our vows. I thought long and hard about what I would wear, where we would do it and who would officiate this special occasion. After multiple shopping trips with my BFFs, I found a dress that made me feel happy, nothing as ornate and tricked out as what I wore in 1988; the dress I selected for this evening was flattering and perfect for this renewal of our life together. Ironically, the dress had a low V-cut back, just like my original wedding gown, but, unlike then, it would now reveal my scars from my lung cancer journey. It had been 10 years since this surgery, but now, quite frankly, I was OK with showing these scars because I had grieved them, and they were a part of my life, my story. I owned and wore them proudly. It had taken some time, but I was at peace with this, as well as all the other difficult hurdles I had encountered.

I was elated to have my sons, Greg and Jordan, walk me down the aisle to meet the only man I have ever wanted to be married to and spend my life with. Over the years, Dan and I had shared, experienced, and worked through all that life put in front of us: great times, normal uneventful days, milestones, and, in our case, moments of significant adversity. I still get emotional when I look deep into his eyes and see his love for me and feel the same profound feelings back because we were the only ones who knew what was going on in our house during our most difficult journeys—and the choices we made to come through them.

77

THE RENEWAL – JUNE 5TH, 2018

Our brother-in-law Bruce officiated the service, which was beautiful. We didn't have a bridal party, but did have our two grandnieces Lia, now two years old, and Maea, now one, walk down the aisle before me, spreading rose petals. It was held on the beach in Long Branch, New Jersey. When I was trying to decide on a venue, Dan said to me, "The beach has always been so soothing to you, your happy place. Why not have it there?"

"That's a great idea!" I replied, and I quickly dove into the plans to make that happen.

I cried when I walked down the aisle, arm in arm with my two sons, now 23 and 26, as I was so proud of these young men, my boys—so beautiful, caring, intelligent, and successful. They were the most wonderful gift we'd received during our 30 years together.

I held Dan's hands, and we locked eyes. I felt that same stir inside of me that I had during our original exchange of vows. How could it be that he still evoked these emotional feelings within me so many years later? I didn't know, but he did. When it came to the vows, "for richer, for poor, in sickness and health" I thought I might cry, but I didn't. I truly understand now, based on what we've experienced, the significance of this bond we made long ago and how important it was, and is, to us, Daniel and Rosemarie, to honor our commitment to each other.

I had learned that I need to stay in the present moment and not worry about what might come during the next phase of our journey together. I needed to focus on being happy, alive, and, self-caring. I needed to have fun and not take myself too seriously. That was especially essential now. And if curveballs came our way, I was hopeful that we had both learned how to handle and attack them one-at-a-time, day-by-day, connected to each other as a team, until we could make it through them without the fear and anxiety that we experienced in years past.

In a traditional Jewish wedding, after the vows and rings are exchanged, the groom steps on and breaks a glass to officially confirm that the couple is married. Even though our brother-in-law Bruce is not a Rabbi, but an ordained minister, and I'm Catholic, Dan wanted to include this tradition into the ceremony, as we did in 1988. After we exchanged vows, Dan broke the glass, and everyone yelled "Mazel tov!" Then we kissed, and our family and friends clapped. I looked back at the attendees and smiled, knowing that everyone there were people who Dan and I deeply loved.

Breaking the glass was a timeless custom in a Jewish ceremony, yet, when it shattered, it made me think about my dear friend Marianne, who told us many years before that, when a glass breaks, it was one of the many ways she would let us know that she was with us. Although today's glass breaking was deliberately done and not exactly how she shared that hers would occur—accidentally—I hoped that she was present that day. I really wanted her to be there, especially since she had been so present during my journey, and so pivotal in my healing.

78

UPDATE ON MOM

I went to visit my mom today. When I arrived at her place, she was gathered around the table at her social hour speaking with her friends. I pulled up a chair to sit next to her and kissed her hello. The residents were in good spirits, sharing stories and laughing. This made me happy.

My mom leaned over and whispered in my ear, "You see that woman over there," and she pointed to her, "she's always complaining about this place. She's never happy. I don't know why she's so unhappy. I like it here—they serve nice meals, I have a three-room apartment, and they keep us busy with activities." I scanned the room and looked at all the resident's faces —my mom's friends—and I smiled. I held my mom's hand and kissed her on the check and said, "I'm happy for you mom, you made the right decision to come here." I turned my face away for a moment to wipe away the tears in my eyes. It's taken quite some time, but I think she has finally settled in.

79

LIFE COACH ROSIE!

This is my vision for my future. Dream along with me... I was in the Green Room, my makeup was done, and I was sitting with Dan, Maribel, Noreen, Geri, Lori, Annie, and, of course, my boys. Someone very official looking popped his head in and said, "We're just about ready for you. I'd say you're on in five minutes." My stomach lurched a little, and I wondered whether I could pull this off. I started to think of all that I had learned from meditation and my public speaking training. Then I put myself into a mini-Master Class to pull myself together. I did a bit of self-talk to convince myself that, "I got this," something that Dan, Greg, and Jordan had told me countless times before, when I was facing my most difficult situations.

I asked this guy, "About how many people are in the audience?"

He said, "I'm not great at numbers, but I heard someone

who is in charge of ticket sales say we're at full capacity, which is about 1,000 people."

My heart pounded a bit harder. I used the breathing techniques I'd learned from meditation to take me back to where I should be. I did some more self-talk to remind myself of why I was here and what I intended to accomplish with the people who had taken time out of their busy lives to be here tonight.

When we got to the one-minute mark, I pulled back the curtain ever so slightly to see what I was up against, but I couldn't see much because the lighting was so bright. Curiously, I was able to see the people in the first row, and I saw Dan, my kids, and both sides of our entire family, cousins, nieces, and friends, now comfortably seated along with my therapist and my breast and reconstructive surgeon. They took up all three sections of the first row, and, while I initially thought I would feel apprehensive, having all of them there, I was stoked that they were with me.

The audience started chanting, "Life Coach Rosie" followed by five consecutive claps over and over and over in sync. Someone sent me a cue that it was time. I heard my favorite Latin/Zumba song come on, and I took a very deep breath in and out, parted the curtain, and did a combo salsa and then bachata dance onto the stage because this felt like a fun way to make my entrance, particularly after all I had been through and how important it was for me to be there tonight. As I sauntered onto the stage, I felt the dime bouncing around under my foot in my left shoe, another reminder of why I was there and what I was doing.

It had taken a bit of time, but now I was ready to spend time with my people, the people who'd been following me via social media and YouTube, and tell my story—what I had learned and what I could give them as a takeaway that, perhaps, would help them make the meaningful changes I had to learn so I could continue on.

Someone in the audience yelled out, "We love you, Rosie."

I responded, "Thank you! I've waited so long to be here with you, and I love you too." I took a deep breath, touched my earrings, Marianne's earrings, and looked up to the sky for encouragement from her and Carl. This gave me the confidence to move forward with my conversation with my audience. I started with the question, "How many of you have experienced significant struggles, challenges that you just couldn't figure out how to get through on your own?"

Three-quarters of the audience raised their hands. Then I shared my story, what I did, good and bad, and how I eventually mapped a plan for how to transition from being in the deepest, most despondent place to emotional wellness, thriving instead of just surviving. And we were off to a meaningful exchange for two hours with, to my delight, very positive feedback from audience members and the media the next day. Powerful and inspiring stuff.

I find this quote to be very inspirational:

> *"One day, you will tell your story of how you've overcome what you went through, and it will become part of someone else's survival guide."*

80

THE NEXT DAY

I woke up this morning, looked at Dan sleeping soundly next to me, and I snuggled up next to him, feeling a sense of peace and contentment. Perhaps I had finally found what I wanted, the answer to why God wanted me to stick around after two cancer journeys, my brother's sudden death, and my mother's decline as she slipped away from us via one of the most awful diseases, dementia. It was the ability to share what I have learned on this journey, to be helpful and inspire others by my story, and the tools and methods I had implemented so that they, my followers, could obtain what I have achieved, and that is to ultimately, *Find their joy and run with it.*

EPILOGUE: MARIANNE

*L*ater in the day, I went out on the deck to meditate, which was something I liked to do when the weather was nice. I lay down on one of the lounge chairs, selected Andy's meditation app, and settled in to get started. When I looked up at the sky, there were at least 10 dragonflies dancing above my head—none in anyone else's backyard—just in mine! I yelled for Dan, Greg, and Jordan, who were home at the time, to come take a look. "Can you believe this?" I said to them. We all stood for several moments in awe, watching them moving around, over and above us. Jordan tried to take a video, but, unfortunately, it didn't come out clear due to the beautiful, ambitious flurry of their activity.

At that point, I had a thought I had to share with my family immediately: "Maybe our guardian angels don't want to be seen via a video that you might share with others. Perhaps they only want their intended recipients to feel their presence." I took a deep breath in, touched my earrings once again, and silently acknowledged my friend and the blessings she has bestowed upon me. This moment was so beautiful. You just can't make this shit up!

ABOUT THE AUTHOR
ROSIE MANKES

*R*osie Mankes has been certified as a professional Life Coach since April of 2016. After her second cancer diagnosis, having had lung and breast cancer, her passion became helping people that are experiencing adversity to move to emotional wellness. Rosie is also a Motivational Speaker and published blogger.

In addition to working as a Life Coach and Motivational Speaker, Rosie has worked in cause marketing connecting senior-level Fortune 500 company executives with non-profit organizations to create win-win partnership opportunities. Most recently, she represented the global non-profit organization Save the Children.

To contact Rosie:
    Phone: 732-817-0849
    Email: lifecoachrosie@gmail.com

Website: https://www.rosiemankes.com

Follow Rosie on:
- Instagram: instagram.com/lifecoach_rosie/
- Facebook: facebook.com/lifecoachrosie/
- LinkedIn: linkedin.com/in/rosie-mankes-0111b811

Made in the USA
Middletown, DE
18 October 2020